For Margaret
God bless
your own
Promises To
Keep
Fr Miles

PROMISES TO KEEP

*People, Places and Parables
in Communications
from around the World*

by
Fr. Miles O'Brien Riley

Other Books by Fr. Miles O'Brien Riley:

With A Song In My Ark
The Impossible Mission
Ikthus
Getting The Good News on the Evening News
To Whom It May Concern
Gift of Love
Your Communication Plan
Training Church Leaders For TV News Interviews
Set Your House In Order
Invo's & Bene's

PROMISES TO KEEP

© Copyright 1991 Miles O'Brien Riley

ISBN 0-9620554-1-7

Design by Jeannette Mahoney

Graphics, layout and typography by
Perfect Page Desktop Publishing
P.O. Box 1963
Orinda, CA 94563

Printed by
Wicklander Printing
1550 S. State Street
Chicago, IL 60605

Acknowledgements

I thank God for these special friends and co-communicators without whom I could not have kept my promises:

Jo Aguirre; The Archdiocese of San Francisco; Kathi Beerbohm; Ed Cavanaro, Dore Culver and KCBS Radio; The Priests, Sisters and People of St. Catherine's Parish; The Catholic Communications Campaign; The Catholic Communications Center, San Francisco; Camille Franicevich; The Priests, Sisters and People of St. Gabriel's Parish; Joan Holmes; Don Ludolph; Pat Medina; Deacon Bill Mitchell; Charlotte Pace; Archbishop John R. Quinn; Dr. Dave Ramsey and the Archives of Modern Christian Art; Bill and Adalene Riley; my sisters — Anne and Ranny Riley; my brothers — Bill, Pat, Tom and Jim Riley; Father Harry Schlitt; Sr. Veronica Skillin, SND; Faculty, Staff and Student Body of College of Notre Dame; and Evelyn Zappia.

Special thank you blessings for the hundreds of missionaries and Catholic communicators worldwide who offered gracious and inspiring hospitality.

Our gratitude to so many kind and generous authors, publishers, photographers, syndicators and fellow Catholic communicators for permission to reprint their valuable work for you here! We are especially grateful to:

> **Gujarat Sahitya Prakash Publishers** and Fr. X. Diaz del Rio, S.J. of Gujarat, India for permission to quote from Fr. Anthony de Mello's wonderful anthologies of spiritual stories.

> **Universal Press Syndicate** of Kansas City, Missouri for permission to reprint the Doonesbury copyrighted cartoon on Korea.

> The **Concise Earth Book World Atlas** and my other references and resources for maps, population profiles and background material worldwide.

> **Wyrick and Company**, Charleston, South Carolina for permission to borrow from Richard Lederer's **Anguished English (Dell Publishing**, New York, September, 1989).

And to the following postcard publishers and distributors, for permission to reprint their cards:

> **Gustra Cards**, Koes Studio, Bali
> **National Palace Museum**, Taiwan
> **Caines Jannif, Ltd.**, Suva, Fiji
> **Postales and Revistas**, South America
> **E. Eismann**, South America
> **Los Kankitas**, South America
> **Herst, u. Verlag Schoning & Co. & Gebruder Schmidt**, Germany
> **Moni Bookshop**, Africa
> **Mt. Kenya Sundries, Ltd.**, Africa
> **Kashmir Crafts, Ltd.**, Africa
> **New Horizons**, Africa
> **Zambia National Tourist Board**, Africa
> **Wirui Press**, Oceania
> **Roki Post Kad**, Oceania
> **Colourview Publications**, Oceania
> **Nucolorvue Reproductions Pty, Ltd.**, Oceania
> **Thomas Vaz**, Goa

Fr. Miles O.D. Riley

TABLE OF CONTENTS

TABLE OF CONTENTS

FORWARD

After twenty-five years of priesthood and twenty years in the mass media ministry, I took a sabbatical year, Easter '88 to Easter '89, to learn how the church in other countries and cultures was using communications to evangelize. I wanted to visit Catholic Communicators worldwide; to learn from their successes and slips, to peek over their shoulders without getting on their backs. I wanted them to see me as a resource — not a distraction.

I began my journey by sending this letter to Catholic Communicators worldwide:

> Fr. Colm Murphy, Secretary General of UNDA International, has asked me to contact you immediately to see if there is some way I might be of service to the communications ministry in your area.
>
> Archbishop John Quinn of San Francisco has granted me, as Director of Communications, a one-year sabbatical to travel the world learning how others use the mass media to evangelize and offering to train or consult where I might help.
>
> In recent years, I have conducted training workshops for bishops and church leaders (using video cameras and interview exercises and guideline workbooks) in the Philippines, Canada, Ireland and throughout the United States. I would be happy to collaborate with you in creating training workshops for the church leaders and communicators in your area.
>
> Please forgive my boldness. I really most want to visit your country and culture and learn what you are doing in mass media evangelization there—but I do not want to come empty handed. I want to offer my services as your brother in Christ. I would appreciate hospitality, if possible, but I need no fees or travel expenses. I have applied for a grant to cover all costs.

Fortunately, two years earlier, two brilliant Jesuit communicators in the Philippines, Fathers Jim Reuters and Jean Desautels, had brought in a team of four to conduct training workshops for the Filipino bishops. Archbishop John Foley, President of the Pontifical Council for Social Communications in Rome, handled papal documents; Bishop Agnellus Andrew, founder of the National Catholic Radio and Television Center at Hatch End in London, taught radio; Fr. Anthony Scannell, OFM, President of the Franciscan Communications Center in Los Angeles, emphasized the creative use of the audio visual materials; and, as Director of the Catholic Communications Center in San Francisco, I focused on the church's need to tell the Good News on the evening news.

Less than two weeks after our workshops the "peaceful peoples' revolution" replaced twenty year Filipino dictator Ferdinand Marcos with elected President Corey Aquino. A dictatorship armed with the two weapons many in the world still think most powerful — economic wealth and military force — was overthrown by a people of hope armed only with prayer and alternative mass media, the church's "Radio Veritas" and sixteen short wave radio stations. It is now history: money and military might were defeated by faith and communications.

Word spread. Invitations to conduct similar training workshops arrived from India, Africa, Europe. My original plan was to spend a month in each of twelve countries — training for perhaps a week and then traveling, learning, and relaxing for the other three weeks. Soon over 50 firm invitations had been received and the plan changed to a week in each country: half teaching, half learning.

That's about how it worked out. As my post-journey report described:

> A sabbatical year, April 9, 1988–April 14, 1989, gave me the unique opportunity to visit 47 countries on 5 continents: to learn how Catholic communicators around the world are using the media to evangelize. In return for hospitality, I gave training workshops for local church leaders, most often the bishops and major superiors of religious in each country.
>
> The workshops were organized in this way: I would arrive in a country on Sunday afternoon. My hosts, typically the communications coordinator for the national episcopal conference or the diocesan directors of communications, would brief me on the workshop's participants and the major pastoral needs and the particular emphasis of their workshops: usually how to use radio, television and print — both secular and ecclesiastical — to tell the Good News.
>
> On Monday we would prepare the conference area and studio space for the workshop and train our crews: videographers, audio engineers, journalists, interviewers — whatever professional talents were

needed. The next three to five days we would conduct an eight-hour-a-day practical communications workshop for 15–25 religious leaders. In addition to these full-day sessions, I also met with small groups for one to four hour seminars and conferences in media ministry.

During the entire year I had the honor to conduct:

–105 full-day workshops for 1,342 people
– 376 conferences and seminars to 6,083 people

Circling the globe several times allowed me to serve as animator or facilitator for three continental conventions:

UNDA-OCIC (Catholic World Associations for Film and Broadcast) Oceania (Samoa, June)

AMECEA (Consortium of Seven Countries of East Africa) East Africa (Nairobi, August)

UNDA-OCIC Asia (Macao, September)

My broad itinerary included:

April/May: England, Italy, France, Germany, Belgium, Netherlands, Denmark

June: Samoa, New Zealand, Australia (Melbourne), New Caledonia

July/August: Zimbabwe, Malawi, South Africa, Zambia, Kenya, Zaire, Ivory Coast, Liberia, Sierra Leone, Mauritania

Sept–January: Korea, Japan, Taiwan, Hong Kong, China (Beijing) Macao, Thailand, Bangladesh, India (Calcutta, Madras, Bangalore, Hyderabad, Bombay, Goa, Cochin), Singapore, Malaysia, Indonesia (Jarkarta, Yogyakarta, Surabaya, Bali)

February: Fiji, Papua New Guinea, Australia (Sydney), Cook Islands, Tahiti

March/April: Venezuela, Colombia, Peru, Bolivia, Chile, Argentina, Brazil (Sao Paulo, Rio)

To make it possible for me to travel for 53 weeks to 47 countries — almost 3 times around the world with cutbacks and criss-crosses — many generous sources contributed finances.

The Archdiocese provided $15,000 for my sabbatical. The National Catholic Communication Campaign gave $9,600 toward the cost of the workshop crews, materials, and equipment. KCBS Radio supplied $8,000 for long distance telephone charges and, in return, I called in a weekly exclusive radio report from each country called "Miles To Go". I sold my car for $7,000 and received $6,000 in gifts. The remaining $17,000 in expenses came from personal savings.

Without detailing every expense item, here are a few you may find interesting:

Air Fare	$19,441.68
Telephone	9,476.57
Room & Board	10,539.92
Staff Fees	4,083.65
Mail & Postage	4,564.77
Audio-Video Equipment	2,613.64
Workshop Materials	2,125.20
Gifts & Contributions	4,693.30

Clearly, a global journey like this would have been impossible without the gracious hospitality of literally hundreds of generous hosts, who gave me much more than free room and board, studio and hardware access, and support staff. Countries as large as India and as small as the South Pacific Islands have such a sacred cultural tradition of goodness to guests that they would pay for all needs: including shopping trips for clothing, toiletries, medicines, and countless gifts — a loving largesse I had never experienced before!

My life has been enriched, personally and professionally, by many beautiful people. It is impossible to make a pilgrimage like this and simply return to "business as usual." Students you can say goodbye to — friends you must see again. I look forward to seeing and serving these special friends again. I promised them that I would tell their story to others and later, tell them how others are using the mass media to evangelize. Last year I had "Miles To Go." Now I have "Promises To Keep."

INTRODUCTION

"A Promise Is A Debt"
(Swahili Proverb)

I was blessed with a one year teaching-learning pilgrimage to 47 countries on our shrinking Planet Earth. We called the journey "Miles To Go" from Robert Frost's poem: "The woods are lovely, dark and deep but I have promises to keep, and miles to go before I sleep—and miles to go before I sleep."

I have gone the miles—2 1/2 times around the globe—and now I have promises to keep: promises to the poor of our world who are too proud to beg for themselves, promises to the millions of our brothers and sisters who are trapped powerless in prisons of hunger, injustice, preliteracy, fear, political oppression and hopelessness, and implicit unspoken promises to the hundreds of hospitable communicators who opened their homes and hearts to me and shared their country and culture, their church and communication.

A promise is a debt—and this little book is partial payment on that debt. Another Swahili proverb reminds us: "The greatest good we can do is not just to share our riches with others—but to reveal their riches to themselves." I hope these profiles, pictures and parables serve as both a window and a mirror—to appreciate the beauty of our brothers and sisters worldwide, and to catch a glimpse of our own.

The stories of faith and family, of laughter and love are not mine. They come from vast continents like Africa, huge countries like China and India, and tiny islands in the South Pacific. Like everything else of value in this book, they belong to the world!

MYTHS

The Master gave his teaching in parables and stories, which his disciples listened to with pleasure—and occasional frustration, for they longed for something deeper.

The Master was unmoved. To all their objections he would say, "You have yet to understand, my dears, that the shortest distance between a human being and Truth is a story."

Another time he said, "Do not despise the story. A lost gold coin is found by means of a penny candle; the deepest truth is found by means of a simple story."

This book contains many stories or "Parables" from around the world. None of them belongs to me—I am only the collector— like Jesus' parables about His Father's Kingdom, they belong to all of us!

EUROPE

ENGLAND

A **T A GLANCE** **ENGLAND**
Population: 56,780,000
Capital, with population: London, 6,755,000
Language spoken: English
Literacy: 99%
Faith Expression: Church of England, Protestant, Roman Catholic, Moslem
Currency: British pound
Cities visited: London, Oxford

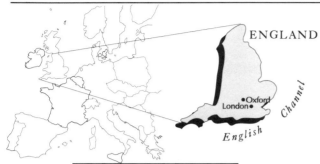

POSTCARD
REFLECTIONS

THE FORTY MARTYR-SAINTS OF ENGLAND AND WALES
from the painting by the General Postulation and executed by Mrs Daphne Pollen

FINDING GOD ON STAGE

In England the first thing you learn is that Protestantism is not the religion of the English — England is the religion of the English. They have a naughty saying in the British Isles: "The Scots keep the Sabbath—and everything else they can lay their hands on. The Welsh pray on their knees — and on their neighbors. The Irish don't know what the devil they want — but will die fighting to get it. The English will all tell you that they are self-made men — and then worship their Maker."

In fact, only 7 million of 56 million people in the British Isles go to church every Sunday. Fortunately, God is alive in the theater. Three Andrew Lloyd Webber musicals which were playing in London sing of our faith. In "Cats," McCavity (evil symbol of violence) wars with Deuteronomy (the God figure), who chooses old, broken-down glamor cat Griselda to be taken up (resurrected, redeemed) through the "heavy side layer" (fog) for a life renewal.

In "Starlight Express" (my favorite—with all the actors and dancers on roller skates!) we are all like trains: steam, diesel, electric, racing through life, competing madly, chugging in circles and only really at peace when we accept ourselves as we are, and believe in the inner power, the starlight express, the Holy Spirit within each one of us.

In "The Phantom of the Opera" a disfigured fellow hides in guilt away from the community, committing evil deeds, living in the dark hole of fear and make-believe, and is redeemed only when he is embraced and truly loved by a young woman confident in her own lovableness.

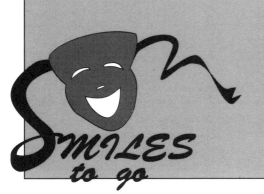

Smiles to go

Question: from a Broadway playwright: "How do I get my leading lady on the front page of the New York Times?"

Answer: "Shoot her!"

When the English playwright Oscar Wilde arrived at his club late at night after witnessing the first presentation of a play that had been a complete failure, someone asked, "How did your play go tonight, Oscar?

"Oh," said Wilde, "the play was a great success. The audience was a failure."

Sheldonian Theatre at Oxford

ENGLAND

As fate and the Holy Spirit would have it, the most wonderful Global Survival Conference was going on at Oxford the week I visited—150 political and religious leaders from all 5 continents. Spent a day with the Dalai Lama, Mother Teresa and Carl Sagan.

Someone at the conference said: "England—such a marvelous climate—and such lousy weather!"

Christchurch, largest and grandest of the Oxford Colleges, seen from the air—the quadrangle was my adopted jogging area.

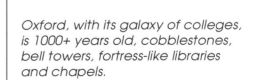

Oxford, with its galaxy of colleges, is 1000+ years old, cobblestones, bell towers, fortress-like libraries and chapels.

THE GLOBAL SURVIVAL CONFERENCE

The first week, I stayed at centuries-old Oriel College, alma mater of John Henry, Cardinal Newman, Sir Walter

Oriel College, Oxford

Raleigh, Cecil Rhodes, et al, participating in the first international meeting bringing together 100 spiritual leaders and 100 political leaders from five continents for a week-long Global Survival Conference. It was the perfect beginning for my year-long spiritual journey to the five continents of our global village.

The Global Survival Conference was kicked off by the Archbishop of Canterbury, ROBERT RUNCIE, who said: "The whole earth is in evident peril. We need awareness of the transcendent. We must affirm the centrality of the spiritual in our various traditions. We are co-creators, with God, of a universe made of love, not cheap or disposable. We need the spiritual qualities of reverence and cooperation for survival." Another speaker said "We must find a place in the budget for the eternal."

DALAI LAMA, spiritual leader of the people of Tibet, said: "We have nuclear power to destroy but also 'love power' to smile, to bring joy, to have compassion. Kindness, the universal religion, is the key to global survival: a reverence for different teachings and traditions. Touching is the most important factor in child development and in human development.

Both the environment and the human spirit are endangered; therefore, we are responsible for one another."

ASTRONOMER CARL SAGAN, of Cornell University, said the two nuclear superpowers' capability to destroy the planet was "like two implacable enemies in a room awash with gasoline, one with 12,000 matches, the other with only 1,500—and they're in a desperate race to get more matches." He continued, "The U.S. and the Soviet Union have booby-trapped the planet with 60,000 nuclear weapons. The U.S. alone has put $10 trillion into its military arsenal since 1945, and the Soviet Union has spent a comparable amount. This is an obscene arsenal." He further reminded us: "You look at all those other worlds in space—and I have examined dozens of them—and you will not find a hint of life. That suggests something of the rarity and preciousness of life."

DR. EVGUENIJ VELIKHOV, vice president of the Soviet Academy of Sciences, suggested that the answer is to reduce nuclear weapons by 50 percent immediately. He compared the arms race to "solving family problems by putting nuclear explosives in every kitchen in the world. It does not work. The nuclear strategy of the last 40 years," he said, "is now recognized as a mistake, the result of our limited scientific knowledge; we simply did not fully recognize the effects nuclear weapons would have on our planet. Now we need a new vision where nuclear weapons no longer threaten humanity."

He questioned President Reagan's Star Wars Strategic Defense Initiative shield. It won't make nuclear weapons obsolete, it's impossible to build, and you'd have to risk blowing up the world to test it. The only answer is total disarmament, which must be achieved by the end of this century. "The key is verification," he said, praising privately funded US-USSR efforts in this endeavor.

One of my favorite participants at the Global Survival Conference was MOTHER TERESA of Calcutta, who reminded us all that "love is the beginning of peace—and love begins at home when we pray together. The family that prays together stays together. Love brings faith, faith brings service, service brings peace." She is fighting abortion with adoption, fighting contraceptives with natural family planning, fighting AIDS with her Gift of Life houses in New York and Washington, D.C.

She told the story of the young Indian couple who brought her the money they would have spent on their wedding—a good deal of money—and said they wanted to share the joy of their love with others. She said, "That's what life is all about: to do small things with great love." She quoted Jesus: "Whatever you do for the least of my brothers, you are doing for me." And she closed, "It's not how much we give, but how much we love."

ENGLAND

CANON PETER BOURNE: DIRECTOR HATCH END TRAINING CENTER

When people say sweetly, "Have a nice day, Father," Peter answers: "No thanks, I've made other plans." Superb host, glider pilot and raconteur, not afraid to ask the tough questions about communications training, like: "How many of our graduates are actually working in the media ministry today?" or "Do you bring Third World students to the training or bring the training to them — in their country and cultural context?" Peter has midwifed a Catholic Media Trust to serve all the British Isles. Here is one important slice of their vision:

The broad principles of action laid down by the Catholic Media Trust include the establishment of local and regional training centers where opportunities for production exist. Instead of training being offered on a general "open-ended" basis, training opportunities will be accurately directed to the opportunities that exist to use the skills once acquired. Thus, when opportunities arise for broadcasting on radio or television, or the making of religious or pastoral video, training will be supplied in the locality, at the level, and with a price tag which can be handled by the prospective trainees.

NATIONAL CATHOLIC RADIO & TELEVISION CENTRE

HATCH END

TV SUNDAY SCHOOL

The biggest Sunday school in Britain is in the studios of *TV-am.* "Sunday Club" is watched every week by up to a million children of all religions or none, of ages between 3 and 14. Rowanne Pasco, the company's religious editor, found TV space to fill before and after Batman when most of the audience were children. She leapt at the chance to break new ground, for there was almost nothing religious for children on television. "Children like action," Ms Pasco says, "and I believe that television should encourage this. Also children express their ideas with such freshness. So I decided to run a programme using as much of their material as I could and encourage them to tell me what they felt about various religious subjects."

One 4-year old drew God with two huge ears ("He has to listen to a lot of people"), one pink for girls and one blue for boys. He also had a very long arm and big hand "to hold out and help the people in the world."

One of the creation stories ran, "Long ago when there was no one about and there was no movement at all, God thought there ought to be some action and it goes on . . . He put some liveness on the world; he thought it all very beautiful because he knew the meaning of it all."

The children have very positive ideas about God and religion. Ms Pasco finds, "Their prayers express their love of God and gratitude to him for all he has made. Nature is a particularly popular subject and everything in it. A national inter-denominational television Sunday school has great possibilities," she says, and she hopes to be able to develop them.

CENTER FOR THE STUDY OF COMMUNICATION AND CULTURE

CREATIVE
COMMUNICATING

A team of religious professionals and Jesuit Catholic communicators in London ask questions like:

- What is the influence of the mass media on religious values and attitudes?

- What is the relationship between theology and communication?

- How do we integrate the study of communication into the training of religious personnel (seminarians, catechists, etc)?

- How do we improve the education of audiences for critical use of the mass media, especially television? How do less powerful minorities in a nation gain greater access to the mass media and become better served by the media institutions?

- What are the ethical responsibilities of media personnel (writers, producers, administrators)?

- How do we develop more equitable international information systems that serve the needs of less industrialized nations and protect their cultural heritage?

- What are the implications of new communications technologies for the Church?

The Center provides:
- A documentation library
- A quarterly international survey and collection of essays
- Research and reference
- Seminars and conferences.

PROFILES
Creative Communicators

MR. JERRY TEAGUE:
Media technical advisor and electronic repairman . . . Works with Fr. Colm Murphy & UNDA to fix the hundreds of thousands of dollars of media hardware worldwide obtained over the years from various grants, now in need of repair . . . Jerry offers a unique, forgotten service especially in developing countries.

MR. JIM McDONALD:
Part of a bright team of thinkers; one of Jim's valuable insights is that communications training in the seminary is not only to help preaching and teaching later on in active ministry—but to improve the seminarians' communications right now, i.e., in-house newsletters, in-service training videos, outreach publications, media education, etc.

ENGLAND

BBC RELIGIOUS DEPARTMENT'S *ENCOUNTER:* A WEEKLY PROGRAM

PRIEST WITH A CAMERA

"People say to me, 'You are a priest, where is your parish?'," reflects Father Joseph Dunn from Dublin. "Well, in fact I have no parish. Then, in another sense I have something bigger than a parish, because my colleagues and I have the privilege of contributing 15 films a year to Irish television. These are shown throughout the country, and the country is our audience, the country is our parish!"

Joe Dunn has been making prize-winning religious documentary films for 25 years during which he has visited over 60 countries often gaining access, as a supposedly simple priest, to dangerous and politically sensitive situations where a more conventional film crew would have great difficulty in penetrating. He is very grateful to have had this unique "opportunity to go outside the Irish situation and to see what may be relevant . . . around the world."

A LITTLE BIT OF HOPE

In New York, some 50,000 people are homeless. Neither the federal nor the city government is coping with the crisis so churches are beginning to get involved. This film looks at the work of Maria Scates, a black real estate agent turned spiritual social worker, who runs the Harlem Ark of Freedom. It's a shelter, which offers 15 men a bed for the night, a good meal, some Bible study and what they have lacked for so long . . a little bit of hope.

SONGS OF PRAISE

One of the British Broadcasting Corporation weekly 1/2 hour shows focuses on ecumenical church prayer and song service, including cutaways to seven interviews at home with Christian families.

"If money is lost, something is lost, if honour is lost, much is lost, if courage is lost, all is lost."

Philip Caraman, S.J.

"The role and responsibility of religious radio and television is to keep the rumor of God alive."

Rev. David Winter, B.B.C.

PARABLE: WHERE IS GOD?

There was once a woman who was religious and devout and filled with love of God. Each morning she would go to Church. And on her way children would call out to her, beggars would accost her, but so immersed was she in her devotions that she did not even see them.

Now one day she walked down the street in her customary manner and arrived at the Church just in time for service. She pushed the door, but it would not open. She pushed it again harder, and found the door was locked.

Distressed at the thought that she would miss service for the first time in years and not knowing what to do, she looked up. And there, right before her face, she found a note pinned on to the door. It said . . . "I'M OUT HERE!"

ITALY

A T A GLANCE   ITALY
Population: *57,439,000*
Capital With Population: *Rome 2,830,000*
Language: *Italian*
Literacy: *98%*
Faith Expression: *Roman Catholic*
Currency Used: *Lira*
Cities I Visited: *Rome (Vatican City), Florence, Assisi, Milano, Venice*

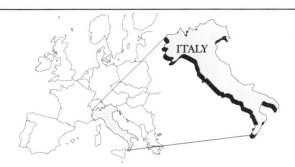

Dateline Rome:

All roads (and catacombs) still lead to the Eternal City and from there back to every part of the world Jesus was dying to save. I went up on the roof of North American College, where I studied when John XXIII was pope, and listened to the churches chime and the fountains splash and the Tiber trickle and remembered the dreams of a young priest 25 years ago, setting out to feed the lonely and touch the hurting and calm the angry and smile at the grouchy. I realized again in this ancient city of earlier Peters and Pauls that we are all part of a great family — big and old — and I felt my hopes reborn and rebaptized with the salty water of tears.

POSTCARD
REFLECTIONS

On a menu:

Our wines leave you nothing to hope for.

In a restaurant:

Special today: no ice cream.

The North American College on the Gianicolo Hill, my home in the 60's, offered spectacular views and hospitality.

View of St Peter's Basilica from my room at North American College.

ARCHBISHOP JOHN FOLEY, PRESIDENT OF THE PONTIFICAL COMMISSION FOR SOCIAL COMMUNICATIONS:
strong background in broadcasting (commercial radio experience as a young man) and Catholic press (editor of Philadelphia's Archdiocesan newspaper for many years), blessed with musical talents, a sense of humor and a commitment to content . . . symbolizes in his person the unity of various media which creative communication requires and which the Vatican (with separate radio, TV, newspaper and press offices) still seeks.

FR. MICHAEL GLYNN:
Irishman, gentleman, has worked with the Pontifical Commission for many years, knows the ropes and the strings and the players . . .

MRS. MARJORIE WEAKE:
kind, fun, smart, loyal, supportive, hardworking feminine power behind the throne in the Pontifical Commission . . .

FR. TOMY LUIZ, SVD:
delightful, generous, helpful, home-based at *Collegio del Verbo Divino in Roma*, edits *Communicatio Socialis*, an annual 300 page journal of Christian Communication in the Third World — the best!

ITALY

PROFILES
Creative Communicators

FR. JIM BERMINGHAM:
gracious, caring, Rome-based communicator, member of St. Patrick's Mission Society and director of Lumen 2000 & Evangelization 2000 in Africa.

Fr. Jim Bermingham

A NEWS SERVICE PROMOTING THE WORLDWIDE DECADE OF EVANGELIZATION
NEW EVANGELIZATION 2000

CREATIVE
COMMUNICATING

LUMEN 2000 & EVANGELIZATION 2000

Lumen 2000 and Evangelization 2000: founded by US Redemptionist Fr. Tom Forrest, director of the International Catholic Charismatic Renewal Office in Rome 1978-1984, and Mr. Piet Derksen, Dutch Catholic businessman millionaire, to evangelize 51% of the world by 2000 AD, especially through the use of electronic mass media. Criticized initially for being too spiritualistic (preaching a devotional gospel without a social justice gospel) and simplistic (our way is the best way — other methods of mass media ministry are inadequate), Lumen 2000 & Evangelization 2000 impressed me in Rome, Singapore, Jakarta and elsewhere as coming of age. They are cooperating with the established local church and communicators, adapting to the cultures and religious traditions of the local communities, open to many creative uses of mass media to proclaim the Good News, and best of all, focused on the Christ-centered faith-content of our message. They are also taking communications training to the various countries (in Africa, Asia, Latin America), instead of bringing Third World Catholic communicators to elaborate training studios in Western Europe or the U.S.

KEYS TO GOOD CATHOLIC COMMUNICATION

These three fun stories describe the essential ingredients of effective religious communication:

1 The priest at the altar suddenly broke into song and chanted: "I am the associate pastor of this parish . . . and I make 400 dollars a month . . . and that's not very much!" The bewildered congregation, wondering if they had changed the liturgy again, began leafing through their missal-ettes . . . When, from over near the sacristy, the old monsignor chanted in response: "I am the pastor of this parish . . . and I make 500 dollars a month . . . and that's not very much either!" The congregation was stunned into silence. A two-beat pause followed. And then, from the direction of the organ loft, came this dulcet melody: "I am the organist of this parish . . . and I make 1200 dollars a month . . and . . . there's no business like show business . . ."

The first ingredient of successful religious communication is not "show biz" but it is creativity and imagination.

2 The young priest was looking out of the Vatican palace when he noticed an unusual sight. Striding across St. Peter's Square was a tall, strong, broad-shouldered man, resembling a carpenter in his long brown robe, hair, beard. With a surge of delight and panic, the priest recognized "Jesus of Nazareth — he's coming this way — what should we do?" He called an older priest over the window: "Eh, monsignore, looka down there villa piazza, Jesus Christ he's acoming thisa way — what shoulda we do?" (It's difficult to translate this joke from the original Italiano!) "I'm only a monsignore — we gotta ask someone piu grande . . . There comes a bishop . . . Sua Excellenza, looka outa the window: Jesus Christ is acomin this way — whata shoulda we do? . . . " The bishop seemed confused: "We gotta tell the Cardinale Secretario di Stato . . . He'sa gonna know whata to do . . . " The three of them hurry down the corridor and burst into the Cardinal's office: "Cardinale, Cardinale, we have justa seen Jesus of Nazareth in the piazza di San Pietro . . . He's acomin' this way . . . what shoulda we do?" The Cardinal reacted quickly: "Men, we go to the top — we gotta take thisa one to the boss!" The four clerics rush to the Pope's private study, where the Holy Father is reading his prayer book. The Cardinal gasps: "Sua Santita, we have justa seen Jesus Christ — he's acomin' this way . . Whata shoulda we do?" The Pope, with a wry smile and a twinkle in his eye, puts down his prayer book, turns to his desk, cranks a piece of paper into his typewriter and begins typing, energetically. The Cardinal Secretary of State can't figure this out.

"But Holiness, whata shoulda we do?" The Pope answered "Looka bizzy! Looka bizzy!"

The second key ingredient of effective religious communication is hard work. Communication is still 10% inspiration and 90% perspiration.

3 He was inspired by the multimillion dollar state lottery to stop by Church. He knelt down and prayed: "Dear God, I have never won anything in my life . . . Please give me a break, just this once, let me win the state lottery. I know I can count on you, Lord, please help me win the lottery. Thanks, God!" And he made the sign of the cross, genuflected and was happily on his way. Nothing happened.

The next day he was back in church, knelt down and prayed: "Yes God, I was talking to you yesterday about the state lottery. God, please give me a break and let me win . . . In fact, God I'm prepared to sweeten the deal: I'll give up smoking and drinking and be kind to my wife . . . Please, just let me win . . . give me a break — I'm counting on you! Thanks." And he left. Nothing.

Third day: Same man, back in church, a little upset with God: "Look, God, I'm not getting through with this lottery request . . . Just this once give me a break and let me win the state lottery . . . " And just then a voice boomed from the heavens: "My son, give me a break: buy a ticket!"

The third, and most important, ingredient of religious communication is faith (accompanied, of course, by good work).

ITALY

THE NEMI DOCUMENT

When I visited Rome in late 1988, the Pontifical Commission for Social Communications was just completing its new pastoral plan for social communications, now endearingly entitled **The Nemi Document**.

PURPOSE: It calls for a vision which incorporates communication strategies in all church ministries. (A personal comment: to dramatize the fact that the Church is Communication—communion is what we are, to communicate is what we do — I have suggested that we close all Departments of Communication, because communication is not just another "department" like "school," "cemeteries," or "youth," — "communication" is our identity and a part of every ministry!)

ASSESSMENT: We must take an inventory of the media situation in each area and/or diocese...the media organizations, media professionals (staff and outside professionals), and resources available: financial, technical, educational and personnel...

AUDIENCE: Next we must ask who we want to reach (our target audience) and how we want them to respond. (A personal comment: often we say we want to reach "everyone" — unfortunately untargeted messages directed to "everyone" usually reach "no one!")

MESSAGE: CATECHESIS, EVANGELIZATION & MEDIA EDUCATION: especially through seminaries, schools and adult education— and through special outreach to media professionals. (A personal comment: I especially like the Nemi Document's emphasis here — in California we are working to establish a special outreach ministry to the Catholic Lay professionals who work in the Hollywood industry and produce 85% of the films and videos seen around the world!)

MEDIA: Press, radio, television, public relations, and service to all...

ACTION: Specific strategies to address social communicational needs...(Please notice some of these areas of action follow-up, e.g. #3, 7, 12!)

1. promote formation of future priests and lay leaders

2. establish professional standards in mass and mini-media

3. educate creative writers

4. encourage and support creative writers

5. develop pilot projects in video and audio cassette production— and collaboration from funding to creative distribution

6. promote relations with media professionals

7. provide pastoral care for media professionals

8. offer media education for parents, teachers, students

9. establish media programs for better media relations

10. present catholic media awards

11. develop strategies for media access to all segments of society

12. design creative patterns for liturgical and sacramental celebrations, adapted to the media and the media generation

13. cooperate with religious congregations working in social communications

14. enhance World Communications Day

15. design and implement communications programs in Catholic Universities

16. organize periodic workshops for church communications in technology and management

17. offer lectures and study days for communicators on ethics and policy issues

PARABLE OF A PILGRIM

There once was an old pilgrim making his way to the mountains in the bitter cold of winter when it began to snow.

An inkeeper said to him, "How will you ever get there in this kind of weather, my good man?"

The old man answered cheerfully, "My heart got there first, so it's easy for the rest of me to follow."

PARABLE OF REVIVAL

Said a preacher to a friend, "We have just had the greatest revival our church has experienced in many years."

"How many did you add to your church membership?"

"None. We lost five hundred."

Even Christians sometimes confuse quantity with quality, membership with commitment!

FRANCE

A T A GLANCE   FRANCE
Population: 55,813,000
Capital With Population: Paris 2,320,000
Language: French (minorities speak Breton, Alsatian German, Flemish, Italian, Basque, Catalan)
Literacy: 99%
Faith Expression: Roman Catholic (90%), Islam (4%)

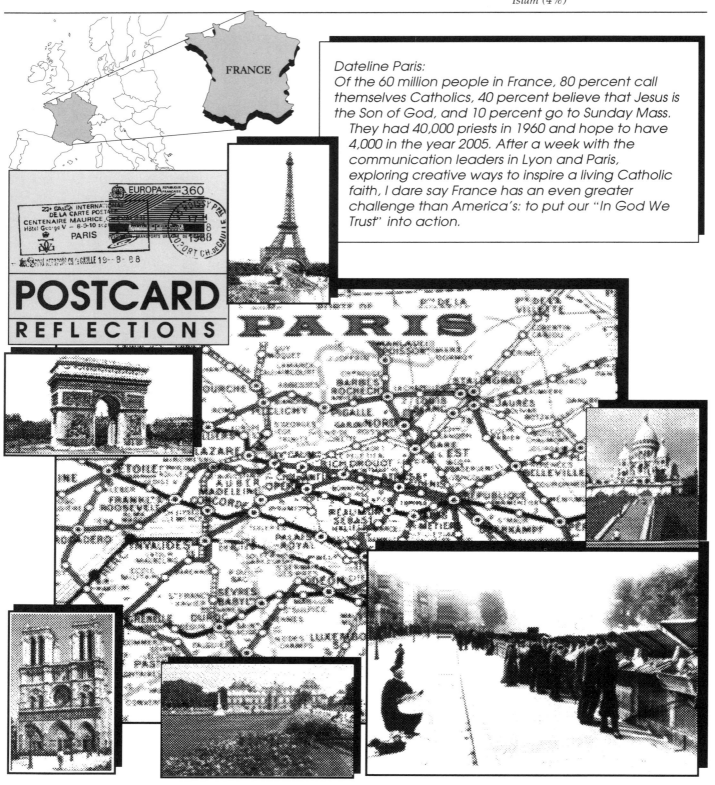

Dateline Paris:
Of the 60 million people in France, 80 percent call themselves Catholics, 40 percent believe that Jesus is the Son of God, and 10 percent go to Sunday Mass.
They had 40,000 priests in 1960 and hope to have 4,000 in the year 2005. After a week with the communication leaders in Lyon and Paris, exploring creative ways to inspire a living Catholic faith, I dare say France has an even greater challenge than America's: to put our "In God We Trust" into action.

POSTCARD REFLECTIONS

In a hotel lobby:

Please leave your values at the front desk.

Outside a dress shop:

Dresses for street walking.

Roman Vestiges in Lyon: The Roman Way

*On the lighter side, Lyon has hills, flowers, glorious food and Father Pierre Babin's media center, **Crec Avex**. Paris has traffic and a pollution-pocked Arc de Triomphe, overwhelming elegance and parfum, and **Bayard Presse**, continental pace-setters in evangelization through the print media.*

FR. PIERRE BABIN: what I will remember longest is not his wonderful training center *Crec Avex*, nor his inspired exploration of music's place in religious communication, nor his brilliant use of graphic visuals in "Photolanguage," but rather his little meditation chapel cell perched on the rooftop of his apartment house like Marlon Brando's pigeon coop in *On The Waterfront*. (Did Karl Malden's *On The Waterfront* priest attract more vocations than Bing Crosby's *Going My Way* priest?)

ODILE TREPPOZ: executive secretary at *Crec Avex* who takes strange (i.e. roamin') priests home to share her lovely, loving family.

Did you hear about the tourist on a rush tour of Europe who screeched to a stop in front of Chartres Cathedral, jumped out and called to his wife, "You take the inside; I'll do the outside. Meet you here in 5 minutes!"

FRANCE

NOTRE DAME RADIO

Owned and operated by the Archdiocese of Paris. The Cardinal gives a ½-hour talk every Wednesday between 7:30 and 8:00 p.m. Bishop Michel Dubost produces daily 60-second **Word of Faith** featurettes defining a religious or church word—actually based on the separation of church and state, avoiding both political commentary/controversy and the "popularization" that French Catholic intellectuals resent. The station broadcasts 12 hours a day.

MINI-TELLE

A communication experiment now 6 years old being used in each diocese in France. 3,000,000 phone terminals, mostly in private homes, pay a phone charge for access to a national data bank, complete with religious information.

LE JOUR DU SEIGNEUR

Under the current direction of P. Gabriel Nissan, O.P., has been active for the past 40 years producing 90-minute shows weekly, with 50 minutes dedicated to presenting a live Mass from a different church in France each Sunday. The remaining 40 minutes allows for a highly produced 40-minute magazine show (these segments are later sold as videos, though not a big seller since only 2% of 60 million homes in France have VCR's, due to the annual high tax on VCR's which supports public TV as well as commercials). With a staff of 30 and a $2,500,000 budget, they are grateful to the 100,000 donors who each contribute a $30 gift two or three times a year. In addition to the 2,000 shows they have produced, they publish a quarterly newsletter.

BAYARD PRESSE

CATHOLIC PUBLICATIONS

BAYARD PRESSE . . . was founded by the Assumptionists in 1873 to evangelize the masses. They began with **Pilgrim Magazine** then in 1883 began a daily paper. From originally distributing publications through parish volunteers, they now have over 1,900 employees and 2,000 contract laborers, with computerized distribution by mail.

BAYARD PRESSE publishes 22 publications, including 9 for children and 3 for seniors, all but one vastly profitable. Of the 2,700,000 subscribers, 2,200,000 are paid subscribers and 500,000 are sold through magazine stands.

La Croix, the only Catholic newspaper in France, developed 40 groups of readers throughout France, to create direct contact with the readers. 100,000 copies are issued daily, with a 4-page middle insert with commentary from readers. It actually loses money but publishers want it to be accessible to the people.

Publications specifically written for the over-50's are **Notre Temps**, **Jeux** and **Vermeil**. **Notre Temps** is not specifically religious in content but provides a service to the elderly on topics such as loneliness, health and pensions, with 1,000,000 copies sold monthly. **Jeux** offers games to keep the elderly intellectually alive, with 130,000 copies sold monthly. **Vermeil** concentrates on reflections of spirituality for the elderly, with 50,000 copies produced monthly.

Children's magazines are graduated by age, with several reading books accenting association between image and word.

In their careful and constant research and segmentation of the market, through audience-targeting, they continue to publish their founding magazine, **Pelerin** (Pilgrim) at 400,000 copies weekly. In addition, to meet the needs of leaders in parishes where there is no priest, **Signes** is available every 2 months (14,000 copies published). **La Foi** is the monthly catechism for adults. **Medias Pouvoirs** (4,000 copies) issued quarterly, lends media insights to politicians, educators and other specialists.

FRANCE

PHOTOLANGUAGE

A picture is worth a thousand — or is it a million? — words! The power of photolanguage comes from the photo and its ability to communicate non-verbal realities like feelings, faith and spiritual experiences.

Photolanguage works like this: you take a hundred or so provocative pictures of human need, emotion, and stories — suggestive photos of world leaders, historical events, or magic moments.

Participants are asked to look through the photos in silence and choose the one that speaks of the conference or retreat theme: e.g. the meaning of our Catholic faith, or communication, or church, or whatever.

When all the participants have selected a photo and returned to their seats in silence, they are invited to share the significance of that picture for each of them. 10 to 15 participants can take turns sharing with the whole group — more than 15 participants can be invited to share one-on-one with their neighbor.

I have used "photolanguage" many times in group discussions, conferences, workshops, retreats — and am always amazed at how this exercise draws people out and enables them to express new spiritual depths.

PARABLE OF GRACE

Uwais the Sufi was once asked, "What has grace brought you?"
He replied, "When I wake in the morning I feel like a man who is not sure
he will live till evening."
Said the questioner, "But doesn't everyone know this?"
Said Uwais, "They certainly do. But not all of them feel it."

Photolanguage — like "media language" — helps us "feel" spiritual realities.

Our Intuition:
audio-visual is not a medium — it's a culture. A new civilization of communication is aborning: we must baptize it.

Our Vocation:
to form a media language and participate in the construction of unity for the universal Church.

Our Identity:
an International Center for Research & Training in Social & Religious Communication founded in 1971 by Fr. Pierre Babin, O.M.I.

Our Mission: .
- Research: of audio-visual language & the new culture
- Training: in new AV technologies for leaders in evangelization
- Production: of books, audio-visual montages & video cassettes.

PARABLE OF HUMILITY

For thirty-five years Paul Cezanne lived in obscurity producing masterpieces that he gave away to unsuspecting neighbors. So great was his love for his work that he never gave a thought to achieving recognition nor did he suspect that some day he would be looked upon as the father of modern painting.

He owes his fame to a Paris dealer who chanced upon some of his paintings, put some of them together and presented the world of art with the first Cezanne exhibition. The world was astonished to discover the presence of a master. The master was just as astonished. He arrived at the art gallery leaning on the arm of his son and could not contain his amazement when he saw his paintings on display. Turning to his son he said, "Look, they have framed them!"

We should all be as talented — and as modest!

GERMANY

A **T A GLANCE**   *GERMANY*
Population: 61,420,000
Capital With Population: *Bonn 293,000*
Language: *German*
Literacy: 99%
Faith Expression: *Protestant (49%),*
    Roman Catholic (45%)
Cities I Visited: *Munich, Frankfurt, Hamburg*
Number of Dioceses: 22

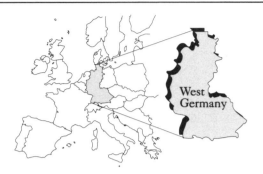

West Germany

POSTCARD
REFLECTIONS

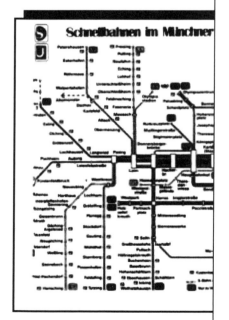

*Dateline Munich:
For evangelizing
communicating,
Germany is in pretty
good shape, largely
because of the mighty
generosity of the
German people.*

*About 50 percent of the population of 62 million are
Catholics, and they contribute $300 million a year to three
special second collections; 8 percent of every German's tax
return is earmarked for religious charity and returned to the
religious denomination of that taxpayer. In Germany the
Catholic Church not only understands the value of the mass
media but also has the financial resources to make a serious
commitment: not to technology and hardware, thank God,
but to training and content — and support for
communicators struggling in the developing world.*

*Munich was the first city where I was arrested. Having missed
my station on the underground railway late one night, I
simply got off the train, crossed under the tracks and
doubled back in the other direction. The secret service
police came through the train and arrested me for having
the wrong ticket on the wrong train and wouldn't believe
my story (or was it my German?). Anyway, they hauled me
off to the station office and ordered me to pay a huge fine.
Since I couldn't explain my way out, I prayed my way out.*

SMILES to go

A sign posted in Germany's Black Forest:

It is strictly forbidden on our black forest camping site that people of different sex, for instance, men and women, live together in one tent unless they are married with each other for that purpose.

PROFILES
Creative Communicators

DR. KLAUS MÜLLER OF SONOLUX:
wide and tender, able to share himself and his beautiful family, a superb trainer and animator who empowers others, ideal for Sonolux's mission to make the local church people great communicators.

The Klaus Müller Family

SONOLUX
International Catholic Group Media Service
Service International Catholique des Média de Groupe
Arbeitsgemeinschaft für audio-visuelle Medien e. V.

Pettenkoferstraße 26
D-8000 München 2
Germany/Allemagne
Tel. (0 89) 51 62 321
Telex: 524 743 lmv d

Fr. Dr. Miles O'Brien Riley
Catholic Communications Center
441 Church Street
San Francisco, California 94114-11793
USA

Munich, 21 April 1989
M/V

Dear Miles,

Let me welcome you back home very cordially. Your last postcard from Rio de Janeiro was a loving sign of your great friendship for which we thank you very much. Yes, my family remembers very well the short days when you stayed with us in Grobenzell, right at the beginning of your global round trip. Even in the memory of Johannes and Mathias you have a firm place as they remember very well the exciting football match we played on the flowered meadow at the little lake.

What a tremendous experience you must have gained after your one year long round-trip. I think you should no longer be called "kilometre" but "globe." I congratulate you to your courage, your strength, your flexibility and your deep humanity that opened so many doors for you and made you so many friends around the world. Your global journey was and is an unique communication experience as you exposed yourself to so many different countries, cultures, languages, people, customs, climates, food, etc. But in all these differences you may have found on a deep, real personal level a common understanding. I imagine it wonderful and enriching to learn from your global experiences. I don't know how but maybe you could think about some ways to make available your experience to a wider circle. Maybe you could tell some stories on an audio tape (or video tape). This would be more lively and fascinating than an old-fashioned written letter. But first relax and enjoy the fascinating feeling: Being at home.

Many blessing and love.

Klaus

GERMANY

The Catholic Media Council

CREATIVE
COMMUNICATING

The Catholic Media Council (CAMECO) was created in 1969 after extensive deliberations between different Funding Agencies and the three International Catholic Media Organizations: UCIP (Press), OCIC (Film), and UNDA (Radio and Television). It is a registered association according to German law, and members of the legal body are, in equal number, representative of the Catholic media organizations and the Catholic Funding Agencies, as well as independent communication experts proposed by the Central Media Office of the German Bishops' Conference.

The main objectives of the Catholic Media Council are:

—to evaluate and coordinate communication projects from developing countries submitted to Church Funding Agencies in the Western World.

—to advise communicators from developing countries on all questions concerning project planning and execution. Assistance is given not only to individual project holders and institutions, but also the Commissions for Social Communications of national, regional or continental Bishops' Conferences.

—to promote cooperation and coordination with other Christian media organizations and Funding Agencies on an ecumenical basis, as well as with International secular media organizations and Funding Agencies for developing countries. Great emphasis is placed on an overall integrated and balanced media policy.

—to collect and collate relevant data on communication and media in developing countries.

G ermany enjoys several helpful services for media ministry.

T he Communications Training Institute in Munich was established in 1969 to train journalists (15 students a year are trained in journalism and philosophy) and now trains German bishops. 10 of the 70 German bishops have taken a media course in the last year, including exercises in telephone interviews, studio interviews, press releases, statements and press conferences.

T he Institut für Kommunikation und Medien (IKM) is an academic department of the Hochschule für Philosophie in Munich. The former was founded in 1976 by Jesuits from the German Assistancy.

It is a goal of the IKM to provide a meeting ground between scholars of philosophy and theology on the one hand, and communication experts and creators on the other, both on the national and also the international levels. The IKM offers Church and non-church communication experts a platform for dialog.

The IKM offers courses and workshops, research, production of radio and TV, audio slides and video and publications.

Dia Dienst Slide Services

For catechetics, liturgy, meditation, instruction and education slides are used in group discussions with children, youth and adults in church, school and community.

Color slides are organized in 5 themes and 25 index words:

1. nature	2. human being	3. environment	4. religion	5. miscellaneous
1.1 cosmos	2.1 body	3.1 culture	4.1 symbols	5.1 biblical themes
1.2 elements	2.2 age	3.2 technology	4.2 natural religions	5.2 Jesus Christ
1.3 landscapes	2.3 situations	3.3 civilization	4.3 major religions	5.3 churches
1.4 plants	2.4 relationships	3.4 profession	4.4 world religions	5.4 religious figures
1.5 animals	2.5 people	3.5 society	4.5 groupings	5.5 religious life

- **Dia Dienst** offers the opportunity to compose your own slide-series.

- **Dia Dienst** facilitates the organization or the systematic completion of your individual archive.

- **Dia Dienst** offers a large variety of motives and provides incentives for creative compositions.

- **Dia Dienst** does not provide complete series of slides, rather a selection from its five theme collections. This makes possible ever new variations of slides with music and words.

- The given structure of 25 index words enables the quick selection of any wanted motive.

- Individual slides can be integrated easily into the **Dia Dienst** system.

- The transparent cassettes can be used in many ways: for exposition at conferences, for a slide archive, for mailing of transport of slides.

- Each edition is accompanied by written material which provides suggestions for slide compositions and methodic-didactical instructions concerning the usage of slides and technical information (in German).

Dia Dienst distributes in the U.S. through the Franciscan Communications Center in Los Angeles.

GERMANY

WOMEN

CHILDREN

Katholische
Presse Gesamtverzeichnis

Information
Orientierung
Lebenshilfe

The German Catholic Press publishes, for
a variety of readers, an enormous number
of magazines and periodicals, a few of
which are shown here.

MISSIONS

NATURE

PARABLE OF GOD'S GARDEN

Goldberg had the loveliest garden in town and each time the Rabbi passed by he would call out to Goldberg, "Your garden is a thing of beauty. The Lord and you are partners!"

"Thank you, Rabbi," Goldberg would respond with a bow.

This went on for days and weeks and months. At least twice a day the Rabbi, on his way to and from the synagogue would call out, "The Lord and you are partners!" until Goldberg began to be annoyed at what the Rabbi evidently meant as a compliment.

So the next time the Rabbi said, "The Lord and you are partners," Goldberg replied, "That may be true. But you should have seen this garden when the Lord had it all on his own!"

Germany is still a country of gardens — and God.

BELGIUM

A T A GLANCE   *BELGIUM*
Population: *9,897,000*
Capital With Population: *Brussels 980,000*
Language: *Dutch, French, German*
Literacy: *98%*
Faith Expression: *Roman Catholic 75%*
Currency Used: *Belgium Franc*
Cities I Visited: *Brussels*

Parting is one of life's painful mysteries. We are always saying "goodbye" to those we love: when we move, when we graduate, when we leave home, when we change jobs, when we break up, when we die. I hate goodbyes. I became a priest, in part, to find a love I would never have to say "goodbye" to.

Twenty years ago as a young priest, just beginning in the mass media ministry, I was giving a three-day retreat for 70 seminarians down by the Santa Cruz shore. After Mass one evening as I stood on a cliff watching a glorious orange and purple Pacific sunset, a stranger, passing by on the beach below, picked up a sea shell and wrote in the damp sand near the water's wash in huge six-foot letters: "HELLO BROTHER."

It took him five minutes. I was stunned. We pass by each other every day and don't even nod or smile. But a complete stranger stopped and spent five minutes saying hello to me. There was no one on the cliff to share this magic moment with, so I wrote my feelings in a song, **Hello Brother**.

Once again the time came to risk good-byes and go for the chance to say hello. I would learn more than I would teach. I would grow as a person, as a priest and as a communicator. Other cultures still provide the best education in the world. Also, I agree with astronaut Christa McAuliffe: "I touch the future, I teach."

Let me describe a typical workshop. First, I would train a team of several news reporters, three video crews, technical support staff and production coordinators. Then we would write tough news interview questions for the 20 or so invited bishops, religious superiors and Church leaders. When the participants arrived at the TV studio or university or workshop site, we hit them with our first "ambush interview." Armed with TV camera, lights and microphone, our reporter asked: "Why did you get out of bed this morning? Where did you last run into Jesus Christ? What would you say to a teenager threatening suicide? What would you do if you were elected pope?" We try to get the participants out of their heads and into their hearts, to tell their God-story, their personal faith story — not just information.

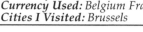
POSTCARD
REFLECTIONS

We would then follow the ambush interview with on-camera practical exposure to in-studio interview shows, press conferences, role reversals where they could interview each other, and more ambush mini-cam interviews. Our 60-page workbook outlines tips and techniques for handling the news media: from strategy to statement, from planning to production to evaluation.

Christian communication is about telling the truth with kindness. Ironically, we preach that the truth will set us free but are reluctant to admit our own sinfulness: alcoholism, drug dependency, sex pathologies, nervous breakdowns, rigidity. We are a Church of forgiveness, but we find it difficult to ask forgiveness.

The workshop was designed to bring out the best in the participants, to enable them to become better communicators with the news media as well as better preachers and teachers.

Take one of our horse-driven city tours—we guarantee no miscarriages.

Hello Brother

Just a stranger on the beach
Just in sight but out of reach
Just the sand and shells to teach
Just another "Hello Brother"

Just a stranger on the street
Just some body on two feet
Just the nerve for eyes to meet
Just another "Hello Brother"

I have nothing I would not share
With someone I thought might care
I'd even risk goodbyes and go
For the chance to say "Hello . . . Brother"

Just a star warm in the cold
Just a smile and hand to hold
Just a "Once-upon-a" told
Just another "Hello Brother"

Just a love when life seems loss
Just a stone without the moss
Just a stranger on a cross
Just another "Hello Brother"

PROFILES
Creative Communicators

FR. COLM MURPHY:
Secretary of General of UNDA. A joy and a jewel, expert and experienced. Knows almost everyone in Catholic broadcasting worldwide—and also knows a few great restaurants and loves to tell good news people stories about who's who, a glue person with a wealth of information . . .

SHEELAGH NOLAN:
the kind of caring, efficient executive secretary you wish worked for not just UNDA but every Catholic Communications Office in the world—since what we communicate (including love and faith) flows from who we are . . .

ROBERT MOLHANT:
Intelligent, organized, dedicated, articulate leader of a superb staff and organization, Secretary General of OCIC, the International Catholic Organization for Cinema and Audio-visual also blessed with artistic sensitivity and a sense for quality religious production.

BELGIUM

CREATIVE
COMMUNICATING

IDEAS IN MEDIA MINISTRY

UNDA . . . which is the Latin word for "wave" is the **International Catholic Association for Radio and Television** with executive offices in Brussels which was formed in 1928 "To accelerate the infusion of Christian values into the media in all its aspects, while at the same time striving for professional excellence in their works." It has as its general aims to insure, as far as possible, a truly human and Christian spirit in all activities of the media, including radio, TV and audio-visual; to help achieve the most effective kind of religious broadcasting; and to promote media training and media education programmes.

OCIC World: **Organization Catholique Internationale du Cinema** is the International Catholic Organization for Film and Video and, oversimplified, is to film what UCIP is to print and UNDA is to broadcast. In fact, all three organizations collaborate closely, especially in the developing world, and are moving slowly toward a practical merger as the sharp differences between the print, broadcast and audio visual ministries begin to fade at the local level: especially as budgets and talents require local mergers of the multifaceted communications apostolate.

PARABLE OF CONSISTENCY

When the guru sat down to worship each evening the ashram cat would get in the way and distract the worshipers. So he ordered that the cat be tied during evening worship. And when the cat expired, another cat was brought to the ashram so that it could be duly tied during evening worship. Centuries later learned treatises were written by the guru's scholarly disciples on the liturgical significance of tying up a cat while worship is performed.

Does this sound familiar?

NETHERLANDS

A **T A GLANCE**   **NETHERLANDS**
Population: 14,689,000
Capital: Amsterdam 994,000
Language: Dutch
Literacy: 99%
Faith expression: Roman Catholic 40%,
    Protestant 35%, Dutch Reformed 19.3%
Currency used: Guilder
Cities I visited: Amsterdam, Baaren,
    Amersfoort, Hilversum, Zeist
Number of dioceses: 7

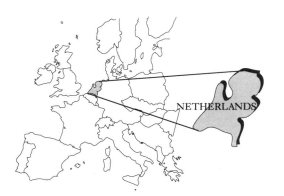

POSTCARD
R E F L E C T I O N S

AMSTERDAM

AMSTERDAM:
City of 700,000 people and
500,000 bicycles: 300,000
bikes purchased each year,
100,000 are stolen and . . .
200,000 are lost in the canals!

A BICYCLE BUILT FOR TWO

At first I saw God as my observer, my judge keeping track of what I did. I recognized His picture, but really didn't know Him. But later I met Christ. It seemed as though life were rather like a bike ride, but it was a tandem bike, and I noticed that Christ was in the back helping me to pedal.

I don't know just when it happened that He suggested that we change places, but life has not been the same since. Apostolic life, that is. Christ makes life exciting.

When I had the control, I knew the way. It was rather boring, predictable . . . it was the shortest distance between two points. But when He took the lead, He knew delightful long cuts, up mountains and through rocky places, at breakneck speeds. It was all I could do to hold on! Even though it looked like madness, He said, "Pedal."

I was worried and anxious and asked, "Where are You taking me?" He laughed and didn't answer, and I started to learn to trust. I forgot my boring life and entered the adventure. And when I'd say, "I'm scared," He'd lean back and touch my hand.

He took me to people with gifts that I needed, gifts of healing, acceptance and joy. They gave me their gifts to take on my journey, our journey, my Lord's and mine, and we were off again. He said "Give the gifts away, they're extra baggage, too much weight."

So I did to the people we met, and I found that in giving I received, and still our burden was light. I did not trust Him at first, in control of my life. I thought He would wreck it, but He knows secrets, knows how to make it bend to take sharp corners, jump to clear high rocks, fly to shorten scary passages.

I am learning to shut up and pedal in the strangest places, and I am beginning to enjoy the view and the cool breeze on my face, with my delightful constant companion, Christ. And when I am sure I just can't do any more, He just smiles and says, "Pedal."

SMILES to go

In an airline ticket office:

We take your bags and send them in all directions.

More than one third of the country lies below sea level . . .

It's no wonder that some Dutch say, "God created the world except the Netherlands, which we had to create ourselves."

NETHERLANDS

Twelve districts are collectively called the "Nederlands," 2 of which are "Holland" (which name is also used to designate the country).

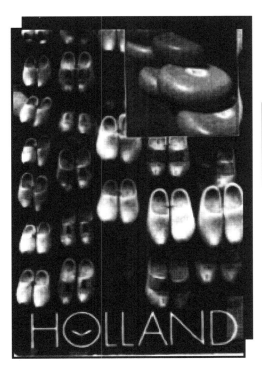

HOLLAND

Wooden shoes are worn by the farmers to work in the canal-drenched fields . . .

The cheese makes Holland the world's largest exporter . . .

FR. HENK HOEKSTRA & MARJEET VERBEEK: give their vision and energy to the Catholic Media Center; typically wonderfully Dutch in their questioning, challenging, discussing the spiritual and cultural values in programs as seemingly irreligious as "Dynasty" or "Miami Vice".

AG LANGEBENT & FRANZ DE SWAAN: on-air personality and executive officer at KRO, personally and professionally dedicated to quality Catholic broadcasting and living the values of friendship and hospitality.

HANNIE VAN DIJK & WILHELMINA MISBACHER: first a warm tender friend, Hannie is also a most gifted and respected college professor who teaches media and teaches about media and teaches with media—together with "MIS" she is the hostess with the mostest!

NETHERLANDS

KRO

The Catholic Radio Organization, now **Catholic Radio and TV Organization**, one of the most interesting and inspiring approaches to Catholic broadcasting in the world, is one of 8 broadcasters in the Netherlands, reaching some 2,000,000 Roman Catholics. In all, the KRO broadcasts 11 hours of television and 68 hours of radio per week. It could be considered the last contact for many Catholics to an association with the Church, a "bridge to both former Catholics and the official church."

The KRO has its own "parish." 150,000 (1% rating) watch Mass from Amersfort, the TV Parish. It is 15 years old, with good liturgy and live congregations. There is a pastoral follow-up with two priests and a sister assigned to this ministry.

It offers 10 minutes weekly for a guest bishop and catechetical instruction and meditations 3 times a week.

625,000 KRO "associates" contribute $60 a year and receive a weekly radio/TV guide (KRO also receives government support and advertising revenues).

CREATIVE
COMMUNICATING

KATHOLIEK MEDIACENTRUM   THE CATHOLIC MEDIA CENTER

Currently directed by Fr. Henk and Marjeet, it offers basic training workshops for 1, 2, or 3 days, charging $125 for a half day for outsiders and $225 for a full day for Center members. In addition, it offers training for non-KRO and non-professionals, especially existing groups, such as pastoral workers, religious education groups, women's groups, broadcasters, editors of parish newsletters and bulletins, providing a media library for course use.

They focus on theology and spirituality and the connection with media/AV and values. Their annual $350,000 budget derives from:

10% course revenues; 50–60% Board participants (for example, the Bishops Conference makes a large contribution); 25–30% from the Dutch Foundation, Benevolencia, with a 5-year guarantee of continued funding and special additional funds for additional special projects. They create many reflective seminars and work to publish articles and reviews which reflect theologically on media offerings.

RADIO NETHERLANDS TRAINING CENTER

Under the current direction of Jim Swaart, the center teaches basic skills in radio and TV, with a full-time faculty of 18 in Hilversum, plus guests, and 6 projects in Latin America. It offers a good program, superb facilities as well as hardware, and is very expensive. Its $3 million a year budget is spent providing courses in The Netherlands, as well as in selected places 'on-the-spot' in Third World Countries, with a strong commitment to media-organization in developing countries which want to use radio, television and the press for the education of their people.

PARABLE OF THE SHOE

A man got into a bus and found himself sitting next to a youngster who was obviously homeless. He was wearing only one shoe. "You've evidently lost a shoe, son." "No man," came the reply. "I found one."

PARABLE OF A BICYCLE

A man left a brand-new bicycle unattended at the marketplace while he went about his shopping. He only remembered the bicycle the following day and rushed to the marketplace, expecting it would have been stolen. The bicycle was exactly where he had left it. Overwhelmed with joy, he rushed to a nearby temple to thank God for having kept his bicycle safe, only to find when he got out of the temple that the bicycle was gone!

Please refer to St. Anthony for lost bicycles (and St. Gertrude for parking places in the city). God is busy with bigger problems.

DENMARK

A T A GLANCE · DENMARK

Population: 5,112,000
Capital With Population: Copenhagen 622,000
Language: Danish
Literacy: 99%
Faith Expression: Evangelical Lutheran 90%, Roman Catholic 6%
Currency Used: Danish Krone
Cities I Visited: Copenhagen

POSTCARD
REFLECTIONS

The disease of our age is loneliness. The problem that causes more headaches and heartaches more than cancer or colds, drugs, divorce, or delinquency is loneliness. It's been a human problem since Adam and Eve got themselves kicked out of the garden, and the problem seems to get worse as we try to crowd more people into one place.

It's almost as if the more we try to conquer loneliness, the lonelier we get. There are people watching TV right now with two or three other people who are lonely. There are other people drinking in bars with a dozen other people who are traumatically lonely. Loneliness is something that happens to all of us from time to time, whether we're alone or with others. It must be part of our fallen human condition.

The ultimate antidote to loneliness is God's love and our faith — our conviction — that we are not alone and our hope that a loving God will save us from our own loneliness. God did that best historically through the life, death and resurrection of His son and the gift of the Holy Spirit of love who dwells with us — and within us — forever.

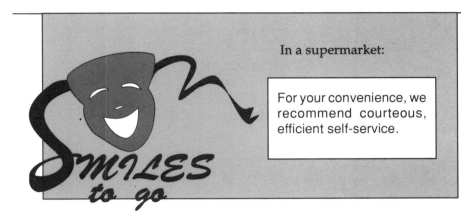

In a supermarket:

For your convenience, we recommend courteous, efficient self-service.

CHRISTIAN TROELSGAARD: One of a team of students for whom video production is a hobby, fascination and possibly a vocation and for whom Dr. Dorn's "KVIP" Chapel bell tower production studio is a godsend.

MERET KLENOW WITH: Catholic lay professional with a talent for writing, producing and hosting radio programs, whose labor of love for the Church creates a weekly radio series as a public service—and who, as a gifted linguist and conversationalist, also hosts a lovely luncheon.

Wonderful Copenhagen

This lovely little mermaid was donated by one of the Danish beer companies—so I'm not sure of the real symbolism. . . but she watches over the Harbor and 5 million Danes and she winked at me when we sailed by.

37

DENMARK

IDEAS IN MEDIA MINISTRY

CREATIVE
COMMUNICATING

Katolsk Videoproduktion

COMMUNICATIONS SUCCESS STORY

The Jesuit University chapel has a 4-story bell tower with a large room on each floor. The rooms on the 2nd and 3rd floors have been converted into a make-shift video production studio and editing suite. Grants and donations help fund the video documentaries; students and video buffs staff the facilities; and chaplain professor Dorn "fathers" the family.

Fr. Dorn sums up their success: "To me the most important aspect of our work is the fact that we as members of a tiny religious minority are managing to break out of our Catholic ghetto by employing video and exploiting the possibilities of local radio which the laws of the land make available for us."

And all this is accomplished by unpaid volunteers!

NIELS STEENSENS KOLLEGIUM

7. januar 1990

Rev. Miles O'Brien Riley
Catholic Communications Center
441 Church Street
San Francisco, California 94114-1793
U. S. A.

Dear Father,
Thank you for your letter of December 4th., which I received a few days ago. The postal service between the USA and DK is rather erratic, so there is no knowing when you will receive this. Maybe much too late, maybe not.

I was away at some international meeting when you were in Copenhagen, but I understand that two of my assistants did meet you and inform you about what we are doing.

. . . .

Of course, the visit of the Pope in June meant that the media focussed on the Catholic Church, but that was just a flash in the pan. Apart from a few retrospective articles in the more serious papers, it was all quickly forgotten.

For us it was memorable for two things.
First, there was our programme on being a Catholic in Denmark. It was made in co-operation with our local Christian (largely Pentecostal) TV and was broadcast on two successive Sunday evenings about what it meant for them to be a Catholic in this secularized Lutheran country. The second evening we had a short film of a family Mass. After this, five telephone lines were open for for questions — they were kept busy for several hours. Everybody was surprised at the response, but then we had made a good video!

The other highlight: in September we started a two-hour radio programme with open telephone. Here the response has been slow in coming, but the number of calls is steadily increasing.

This work with the media has been done entirely by unpaid volunteers. Having the final responsibility, I have inevitably had to bear a large part of the burden. We Jesuits have now decided to employ a man with professional training on a full-time basis for a trial period of three months. We hope in this way to prove to the ecclesiastical powers that be the desirability of having such a media person to work for the whole diocese. We trust we can convince the bishop and the Pastoral Council, because we S.J. will not in the long run have the financial resources to pay his salary.

Best wishes for God's blessing in the new Anno Domini MCMXC.

Sincerely —
L. O'Dorn

PARABLE OF DR. ELEPHANT

The president of a prestigious university, convinced of the Master's mystical experience, wanted to make him head of the theology department.

He approached the chief disciple with this proposal. The disciple said, "The Master emphasizes being Enlightened, not teaching Enlightenment."

"Would that prevent him from being head of the department of theology?"

"As much as it would prevent an elephant from being head of the department of zoology."

IRELAND

AT A GLANCE   **IRELAND**
Population: 3,734,000
Capital With Population: Dublin 503,000
Language: English, Gaelic
Literacy: 99%
Faith Expression: Roman Catholic 95%, Anglican 3%
Currency Used: Pound
Cities I Visited: Dublin

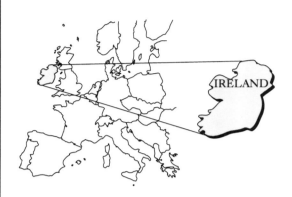

Nearer My God To Thee

On the way back from Ireland, I fell into one of those squashed, straight-backed airplane naps. Two hours over the Atlantic, a flight attendant woke me gently: "Father, I need your help."

"How long since your last confession, " I responded automatically.

She smiled: "Actually, the crew members suggested I talk to you. You may have noticed the row of five kids up near the front of the plane, the very pale children with no hair . . ."

We had all noticed them—and wondered why such frail, sickly kids were on the plane. The flight attendant lowered her voice: "All five are dying of cancer. They have only months to live. These kids want to visit Disney World in Florida before they die. There is a foundation in England, a trust fund set up by a wealthy man, which grants terminally ill children their dying wish. They have all their tickets—but not much pocket money."

I pretended to be upset: "So you have come to me because you want me to take up a collection, right? And you asked a priest because you think that there is something religious about a collection!"

The poor woman was rosy-cheeked with embarrassment. "Well, I, we just thought you would know what to do."

"My dear, you were absolutely right. Collections are indeed religious, and taking up collections is one of the more priestly things I do. Of course, there are a few people who don't like collections, who think they are unsavory, necessary evils, but they don't understand that collections are opportunities to give of ourselves and that money is a powerful symbol of love. I will be proud to take up a collection for the children, on one condition: that I be allowed to use the captain's microphone."

"But, Father, FAA regulations prohibit passenger use of the official speaker system."

"I am not going to walk through this Boeing 747 explaining the situation individually to 450 people. Please check with the captain."

She was back in 20 minutes. "The captain has obtained permission for you to address the whole plane. We are all very grateful to you. But, Father, remember: the children can hear what you say, too."

I got the children's first names and spoke to the whole plane over the intercom: "Ladies and gentlemen, this is not your captain speaking—this is your chaplain! (I didn't want them to think another Miami flight was being skyjacked!)

"I am not going to preach to you today about how flying into the heavens is like the journey of life—nearer my God to thee—even though Jesus promised: 'Lo, I am with you always.'

"But I do want you to know about five very special children who are flying with us on this journey. Their names are Carl, Marc, Craig, Vicky and Donna, and they have received a special dream-come-true: a trip to Disney World. Their tickets are paid for, but they sure could use some spending money.

"If you are Catholic, think of this as a second collection. Otherwise, you are invited to make it an early Christmas. Your flight attendants and I will now pass the baskets which we have borrowed from the first class bread and fruit service and give you a chance to give the kids a love-offering for Disney World."

As we walked down the aisles collecting money, thanking folks and whispering explanations, I watched a group of 450 strangers gradually galvanized by a common cause. A few eyes narrowed in anger, while lips hissed: "How dare you invade my privacy!" But most eyes filled with tears and compassion: most lips spoke blessings and prayers.

One man came back to me a second time: "Here, Father,

Smiles to go

PROFILES
Creative Communicators

this is the money I was saving to get out of the airport parking lot. I'll manage somehow."

We emptied the baskets on the galley tabletop and counted over $1,000 in dollar bills and pound notes and another $500 in coins from around the world. We filled a big plastic ice bucket which I delivered to the doctor accompanying the children. The kids didn't quite understand, but the doctor did, and so did our planeload of happy people who had just become a family.

Near the end of our nine-hour flight, the captain presented me with a copy of the map and flight log signed by each of the 11 crew members as a thank-you card.

My most precious gift arrived several months later. The doctor wrote to tell me about their visit to Disney World. He described each child's favorite ride and favorite animal—and how much life and love the trip had brought to their short lives. He enclosed a photo of our little friends at Disney World, and, I've checked closely, every single one is smiling.

Some Irish Family Names

FR. MARTIN TIERNEY: Director of the **Catholic Communication Institute of Ireland**—quiet, sharp, strong, imaginative leader who has brought video cassettes to the five *Veritas* bookstores. (Actually traveling around the English-speaking world to obtain Irish distribution rights for the best religious videos—and, in the process, dramatically increasing both sales and service) . . . authored **The Media: And How To Use It** (*Veritas*, 1988) practical guidelines for mass media ministry . . . hosts jet-lagged guests at his gracious country cottage and also hosts media workshops for Irish church leaders.

FR. TONY BYRNE, C.S.S.P.: wise, patient, itinerant (mostly in Africa) teacher and author of **Working For Peace & Justice,** a simple practical guide to educate, animate, and get people really working for peace and justice . . . uses Paolo Freire's **Process/Praxis**.

Process/Praxis

Step 1: What does this mean? Silent prayerful reflection, one-on-one sharing, group discussion...

Step 2: Why do you think/feel that way?

Step 3: Teacher's input...

Step 4: The personal and group reflections mixed in with teacher's input...

Step 5: So what? Action follow up!

IRELAND

C.C.I.I.

Sometimes structures help communication. Often, organized unity—one director, one direction—helps each district communications office or ministry improve its service. The **Catholic Communications Institute of Ireland** is both efficient and effective—and includes a publishing division (their 40 page catalog includes dozens of new titles—including inspirational adult education, devotional and psychological self-help and special materials for children), audio and video production and distribution (hundreds of cassettes—many obtained from other English-speaking countries), media training for church leaders, and five retail religious bookstores. Fr. Martin Tierney is the driving—and flying—force behind this quiet development.

CREATIVE
COMMUNICATING

FR. MILES' BISHOPS' COURSE

These special one-day courses, designed specifically for selected lay and religious leaders, teachers and people involved in the media and in media education, consist of workshops on electronic communication, on communications skills and on the effective use of television, radio and the press.

There are two full-day workshops on TV and radio; one full-day workshop on communication; one full-day seminar on media education.

Areas covered in the courses:

- Your communication plan
- Your audience
- Your message
- Evaluation of the media and news
- Interviews and interviewers
- Preparation for interview (planning and polishing the message, preparing yourself physically and spiritually)
- Interview-handling guidelines (introduction, appearance, style, spirit and tone, approach, conduct, and content).
- Tips for handling hostility and exploitation
- Dealing with the press (press kits, press releases, press conferences)

The purpose of the course is to train church and lay leaders in the learned and practiced art of the TV and radio news interview and in dealing with the press, as well as providing basic guidelines for recreating the same training experience in your own diocese, parish, area or school.

From a flyer for the course described on the facing page.

IT'S THE WAY YOU SAY IT . . .

Bishops learn "ers" of their way . . . in front of TV camera

● Miles O'Brien Riley, Ph.D., director of communications for the Archdiocese of San Francisco, speaking at the communications course for Bishops at Carysfort College.

● The Auxiliary of Kildare and Leighlin, Most Rev. Dr. Laurence Ryan, listening attentively during the communications course at Carysfort College.

The Catholic bishops went back to the classroom yesterday to control a growing problem for all potential stars in the spotlight—just how do you look good on TV?

A splendid crusading answer to the pestering television reporter is one thing. But we are talking—if you will forgive the phrase—visual here. That means inserting the M factor. M for media.

"Umms" and "ers" are the kiss of death to credibility. And you had better watch where you are looking. People have got to believe your verbal masterpiece, and who would trust anyone with shifty eyes?

American media specialist Rev. Miles O'Brien Riley from San Francisco doesn't look anywhere apart from straight at you.

He used that professional skill to give 15 members of the Hierarchy the message yesterday at the communications course he

Report: Greg Woodfield
Pictures: Gery O'Gorman

is running this week at Carysfort College, Blackrock, with award-winning TV producer Roberta Cole.

The course is to make sure members of the Church keep pace with the fast moving TV, radio and print journalism world, where an unguarded comment or bad presentation can lead to problems. It includes interviews with leading TV and radio personalities and lectures on the media by senior journalists.

More than 75 Church and lay leaders from all over Ireland are expected to have been drilled in the art of TV when the five-day series of lectures ends.

IRELAND

THE IRISH TIMES, Friday, November 27, 1987

Many bishops burned at the take

By Joe Carroll

Bishops were being ambushed by prying TV cameras in Blackrock, Co Dublin, yesterday and asked questions like: "What would you do if you were appointed the next Archbishop of Dublin?" or "Are you going to excommunicate Gerry Adams?"

The answers, alas, must remain "off the record" as the Catholic Communications Institute, which was running this course on how to make bishops TV stars, could not make up its mind whether it wanted The Irish Times there or not.

A press release had announced that Cardinal O Fiaich and about 15 bishops would be attending a one-day course on communications in Carysfort College. It would be "back to school" for the bishops, the release said, under the expert eye of the Rev. Miles O'Brien Riley, a TV guru from San Francisco.

Then came a follow-up invitation from a senior official to come along and watch, and why not bring a photographer? But when another senior official saw this reporter drinking coffee with friendly bishops, he squawked: "What are you doing here? You are not invited."

Obviously there was a breakdown in communications in the Catholic Communications Institute right in front of the great media expert from the US. **The Irish Time**s generously offered not to report what the bishops said on their trial-by-camera and the replies will remain secret until the year 2087 or the Day of Judgment—whichever comes first.

However, in case Gerry Adams is worried about his spiritual future, he was not electronically excommunicated, although the bishop in question would gladly have excommunicated Anne Daly of **RTE**, who asked the nasty question.

The course turned out to be fascinating stuff. Father O'Brien Riley raised the hair on the heads of our bishops about the kind of questions their counterparts in the US have to face concerning gay priests and even a nun who clobbered her mother to death with a crucifix after seeing "The Exorcist." No wonder **The Irish Times** was not supposed to be there. It was time to make our excuses and leave.

One last snippet from the Index of Forbidden Interviews. Bishops going in front of the cameras are advised not to indulge in "drugs or dating." This does not refer to "taking nuns to the cinema" or "sniffing grass" but, said Father O'Brien Riley, but to—"OK, cut it there, Your Grace."

Irish Parable

The Irish are their own best parable, with a lyrical story telling style to match their magical leprechauns and mythical lore. Tongue in cheek, twinkle in eye, much truth is communicated in the humorous tales of make-believe Patrick and Bridget informing Monsignor McGinnis that they must get a divorce after almost 75 years of marriage. "But you are both over 90 years of age," replies the parish priest. "Why have you waited so long?" Bridget answers, "We had to wait until the children died!"

Sure, and it's a different couple altogether who, in their 70's, approach Fr. Timothy to witness their nuptial vows. Fr. Tim seems surprised: "My dears, you have courted each other for 30 years . . . Why do you suddenly desire marriage?" The aging groom explains: "Father, I'm of a mind to have a little heir!" Father answers: "Well, you may be heir-minded — but I doubt that you are heir-conditioned!"

Apocryphal or not, Irish tales make for good parable-telling. Like the Irishman who spent two weeks at the seaside taking the air and sun — and suddenly died of a heart attack. His tan was still visible several days later as his body lay in the open coffin at the wake. Two little old Irish ladies came up to say a Hail Mary. One whispered to the other: "The vacation did him a world of good."

Erin Go Braugh!

AFRICA

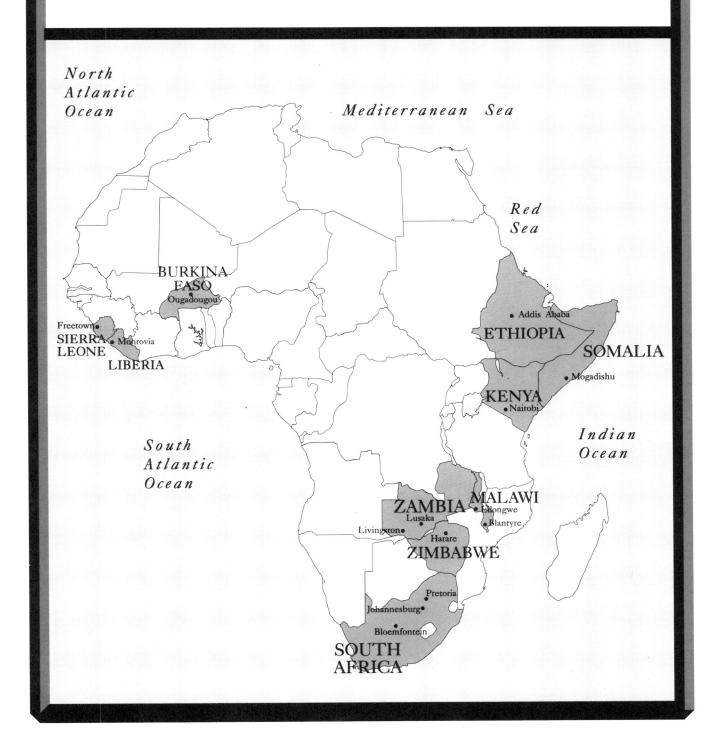

SOUTHERN AFRICA

A **T A GLANCE**   **ZIMBABWE**
Population: 9,987,000
Capital With Population: Harare 730,000
Language: English, Shona, Sindebele
Literacy: 50%
Faith Expression: Predominantly traditional tribal beliefs,
        Christian minority
Currency Used: Zimbabwe dollar

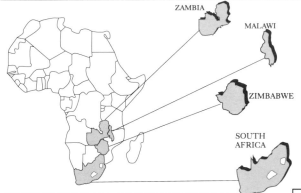

ZIMBABWE

Harare

POSTCARD
REFLECTIONS

Zimbabwe, formerly Rhodesia (from Cecil Rhodes of Oriel College, Oxford!), has 10,000,000 people — with 90,000 Europeans. Tobacco and cotton are big products. Smokers of the world unite—Zimbabwe is the world's second leading producer of tobacco. The stuff is everywhere! Of course, the locals can't afford to smoke so it's exported to feed what remains of our first world addiction! People make $100/monthly—food, housing, education are priorities. Cars cost $40,000, TV's $6,000, VCR's $5,000. One TV station broadcasts five hours in the evening only. Folks focus on priorities like culture, kindness and love.

In a hotel:

In case of fire, do your utmost to alarm the hotel porter.

PROFILES

Creative Communicators

**Harare,
ZIMBABWE**

SR. MARLENE SCHOLZ:
a leader, one of the more experienced, respected and admired religious communicators in Africa: understands how to adapt media ministry to the two most dramatic developments in the church worldwide: Inculturation and S.C.C.'s (Small Christian Communities) — in the communications world called "group media" as opposed to "mass media".

Saved by Celibacy *. . . "I want to marry you," she said matter-of-factly. Asha was a tall, elegant, ebony black Masai woman. We worked together as group animators for a week in Africa. Her sight was dimmed by the relentless African sun, but it was the first proposal of marriage I had received, and for a 50-year-old it was momentarily flattering.*

"Asha, thank you for the compliment, but I am a Catholic priest and I made a life promise to serve God and the Church full-time."

"That's okay," Asha answered spontaneously. "I'm Muslim; we can get married in my faith."

The scenario of introducing Asha to my dad and the archbishop flashed across my imagination. "Ash, God is saving someone very special for you — keep watching and praying." And I thanked God for sending those little surprise affirmations that bolster our fragile egos.

Legs and Life *. . . God also sends little boosts for tired bodies. After one month and five countries in Africa, the old muscles in my back and legs began to ache . . . until one evening when two young boys came running up from the ocean screaming, "Help, help, call ambulance, doctor!"*

Several people were pulling a man from the water. He had slipped off his outboard motor boat trying to start the engine and got his legs caught in the propellor blades. We were 60 kilometers, an unpredictable ferry ride and more than an hour from the nearest town. There was one pay phone available. Someone went to call.

The man's legs were shredded to the bone. He was blue from the shock, the cold, the loss of blood. We made tourniquets from two bandannas and tied them tightly at the top of what was left of his legs to stop the bleeding. A doctor miraculously appeared and gave a medical compliment to our spiritual and human ministry.

After more than an hour, the ambulance arrived, and I prayed that they would catch the ferry and make it into town in time to save his life, if not his legs. They did. But none of us slept very well, wondering and worrying that night. And I remember waking up the next morning with a lot less ache in my back and legs.

Travel is only a visible metaphor for the invisible journey we're all making to find God. Of course, what happens instead is that God finds us — and touches and teaches us through others along the way.

Africans are particularly good at teaching through proverbs. They say: "I pointed out to you the moon and all you saw was my finger." They challenge us to look beyond the finger to the beauty of the moon and also to the beauty of the person behind the finger. They believe: "The greatest good we can do for others is not just to share our riches with them but to reveal their riches to themselves."

SOUTHERN AFRICA

A T A GLANCE   **ZAMBIA**

Population: *7,770,000*
Capital With Population: *Lusaka 900,000*
Language: *English, Bantu dialects (8 major local languages)*
Literacy: *54%*
Faith Expression: *Predominantly Animist, Roman Catholic 21%, Protestant, Hindu, Moslem minorities*
Currency Used: *Kwacha*

PROFILES

Creative Communicators

Lusaka, ZAMBIA

ARCHBISHOP EUGENIO SBARBARO:
Papal Nuncio to Zambia and Malawi, warm, affectionate host, experienced diplomat, committed churchman and creative communicator — who not only organized a 4-day workshop for the bishops of Zambia's nine dioceses, but also used the on-camera exercises to improve his own skills at public reading and speaking . . . May God bless the Church with many more who have his sensitivity, energy, and dedication to communication.

ZAMBIA

Lusaka

Livingston

Livingston, Zambia. Victoria Falls (makes Niagara look like a shower) are spectacular. The roar was soothing to my jangled nerves after 9 straight days of 10 hour workshops. Who said the Africans were laid-back? They're hungry for media knowledge—and taught me much about life.

Zambia has hippos and crocodiles along the Zambezi River which flows into Victoria Falls (300' high, one-mile wide) the most majestic waterfall in the world. Named "MUSI-OU-TUNYA" (the "Smoke That Thunders") it creates triple rainbows. We saw hogs, deer, zebra and a rare white rhino — but no lions! The wild monkeys played at my window and ate bananas from my hand. Jogging the "Bush" was exciting except that the little black children were often frightened by and ran from my white face: I kept forgetting I was white because there were no mirrors . . .

. . . Which reminds me of our visit to the MASAI village where the people had never seen themselves — in mirror or photograph. My companion had an instamatic camera and asked the family to gather outside their simple hut for a photo. They had no idea what was going on. He lined them up, took the picture, waited 60 seconds for the photo to develop, and presented it to the father, who exclaimed excitedly: "Look, there's my mother! . . . and there is my wife! . . . and the kids! Wait, who is this man?" He had never seen an image of himself! What a shock!

Population: *8,063,000*
Capital With Population: *Lilongwe 225,000*
Language: *Chichewa, English, Nyanja, Yao, Tumbula*
Literacy: *25%*
Faith Expression: *Christian 75%, Moslem 20%*
Currency Used: *Kwacha*

MALAWI

Lilongwe

Blantyre

8,000,00 Malawians, 25% Catholic (7 dioceses, 120 parishes), earthy huts, corn meal twice daily, (every family grows maize or corn in the backyard to eat and to supplement $25/month income), extremely hospitable. The border by the big mountains is overrun by 500,000 Mozambique refugees—Malawi struggles to preserve its freedom won in 1964. Gentlest people I've ever met.

The Malawi people are very friendly: I was introduced to almost every person at the Lilongwe Airport — they show respect by whispering, bowing, averting their eyes, and holding their right elbow with the left hand as they shake hands. Unfortunately, women don't know they are equal to men yet — e.g. never joining the men at the family table for a meal.

After death and burial the people celebrate three days and nights of mourning when the whole village gathers to sleep, eat, pray, sing and grieve with the family of the dead. No electricity in the villages, so everyone's in bed by 8:00 p.m. — and up at 4:00 a.m., the crack of dawn — they live in circles of mud huts with thatched roofs.

Two great delicacies: sugar cane and "Malawi sausages" — tiny field mice boiled, dried, sold five on a bamboo stick and eaten: eyes, ears, teeth, tail and fur as a heavenly hors d'oeuvre!

*My name was changed in Malawi. The day I arrived the Archbishop of Lilongwe introduced me to the several hundred people in church. "This is Fr. Miles. He has come to teach the bishops how to communicate better. But we don't have **Miles** anymore in Africa - so we are going to re-christen him **Fr. Kilometres.**"*

PROFILES
Creative Communicators

Lilongwe, Blantyre, MALAWI

FR. DOMINIC MUSASA: patient dynamo, incarnates two of the most important values in Catholic communications: the truth with kindness . . . as executive secretary of the Episcopal Conference he recognizes the importance of training church leaders to tell the Good News on the evening news.

MR. ALEXIUS GODDIA: blessed with a voice rich, mellow and firm and a heart filled with faith, he has dedicated both his voice and his heart to the service of religious broadcasting on Malawian network radio.

"Agogo"—elderly Malawi man

SOUTHERN AFRICA

A T A GLANCE   REPUBLIC OF SOUTH AFRICA

Population: 35,624,000
Capital With Population: Capetown 1,910,000, Pretoria 830,000, Bloemfontein (population n.a.)
Language: Afrikaans, English
Literacy: 99% whites, 69% Asian, 62% "coloureds", 50% Africans
Faith Expression: Christian(DutchReformed/Anglican/Congregationalist/Methodist/Roman Catholic), Hindu, Moslem minorities.
Currency used: Rand

PROFILES
Creative Communicators

Johannesburg, SOUTH AFRICA

FR. DICK BRODERICK:
(also Frs. Oswald, Nick, and the whole LUMKO Team) morning chapel liturgy and evening fireside fellowship are the daily communication "bookends" for this extraordinary group of media missionaries, who are changing South Africa and the world with their faith and workshops, their education and example . . . they practice what they teach — besides, they're fun to live and pray with!

MAGGIE HELASS:
communications coordinator for Bishop Tutu and the Anglican Church: brilliant writer, compassionate Christian, caring friend. Maggie's newsletters, news releases and faxes build bridges of information and understanding.

IMMIGRATION CONTROL: detained at Johannesburg Airport on arrival— examined by 4 different officers (I realized eventually that I represented three of the things they hate most: America, the Catholic Church, and the mass media), who screamed at me: "What do you intend against our government?"

PRETORIA: on arrival I asked a store clerk: "Can you direct me to the center of Pretoria—I'm looking for the South African Airways office?" He answered: "You know where the bomb went off last week . . . it's right across the street!"

SOUTH AFRICA

Pretoria
Johannesburg
Bloemfontein
Cape Town

SOUTH AFRICAN CATHOLIC BISHOPS' OFFICE: Sr. Cecelia Smit received a surprise visit from two young men, in their early 20's, just out of 22 months in prison—"detained" without charges, legal hearings, representations, etc.— simply because they taught catechism! "How many legions does the pope have?" asked Napoleon. Totalitarian governments—from Africa to China, Russia to Latin America—are threatened by religious educators and communicators who have access to peoples' minds and hearts.

Xhosa homestead near Lumko, Transkei

JOHANNESBURG: SABC, South African Broadcasting Corporation, where I spent the entire day visiting with both the television side and the radio side (referred to affectionately by the 7,000 employees as "Sodom and Gomorrah"), offers a nice hot lunch in its cafeteria. When the black server behind the counter missed my order for "rice" the white supervisor behind him hit him on the back and shoved him violently and yelled: "Didn't you hear him? Give the man his rice!"

During the lunch my two practicing Catholic hosts explained that blacks in their parish received Holy Communion from the same cup as whites — but they drew the line at intermarriage. I asked why, if they share communion, they couldn't share the vote. They answered: "Because the blacks would outvote us!"

MY LAST AFTERNOON IN SOUTH AFRICA: we spent the afternoon visiting a middle-aged middle class black couple named Jack and Susan—both teachers, and therefore terribly threatening to the government: Jack had spent the entire last year in prison—no charges, no trial, few friends, only the local parish church to support his wife and 4 children. We also visited the home of a young black family whose father was a social worker. The house had been raided and fire-bombed several times; mom and dad and the two babies were "on the run" hiding out in various friends' homes to avoid being murdered by the soldiers and police; their two daughters, 14 and 16 years of age, were cleaning the smoke off the walls and floors—everything had been damaged and there was no running water or indoor plumbing . . . and I still remember the hopeful concern for their family in those little girls' eyes—and the smell of the smoke . . .

PROFILES
Creative Communicators

Pretoria, SOUTH AFRICA

SR. CECILIA SMIT:
media director for the South African Catholic Bishops' Conference: strong, imaginative, dedicated to the Church, the poor and the struggle . . . creating a new "media unit" of 6 people, a coordinator, information officer, 2 print producers, a documentation researcher and a trainer for newsletters, bulletins, public speaking and diocesan structures — introduced me to the personal side of South Africa's dehumanizing apartheid. Two 24-year old catechists (black) came to visit her after two full years of being "detained" in prison without charges, legal counsel, judge or jury. They "answered" my American disbelief that anyone could be arrested for teaching Jesus Christ by referring me to the gratuitous torture and barbarous infamy of the Holocaust . . . When they were gone I sobbed tears of frustration at such injustice. Gradually I would learn that similar tyrannical governments with terrorist tactics to retain power exist throughout Africa's 50 countries and throughout the world. Sr. Cecilia's media center is located in the Bishop's Pastoral Center named "Khanya House" which means "Light House." May these brave soldiers of peace and justice continue to light their Christ-candles, as well as curse the darkness!

SOUTHERN AFRICA

BERNARD SPONG:
wise, gentle, loving director of the Interchurch Media Program based at "Khotso House" ("Peach House") who makes films, videos, tapes and training seminars for church groups to support the educational dimensions of the Christian's prophetic role and option for the poor. Not long after my visit, "Peace House" was firebombed and destroyed by government officials who were properly threatened by Christians' education aimed at justice and its corollary, peace . . .

KRYSTINA SMITH:
affectionate wife (of a corporate attorney) and mother (of 3 great kids) and music teacher (at the major theological seminary for South Africa) and member of "Black Sash," an imaginative, powerful and helpful group of white women challenging their white government (and families) to bring support to their black fellow citizens . . . I spent my last night in South Africa in Pretoria with this "caring" Smith family, sleeping on their living room floor by the fireplace — while bombs exploded near my earlier residence in Johannesburg . . .

CREATIVE
COMMUNICATING

IDEAS IN MEDIA MINISTRY

LUMKO . . . is an institute of the Southern African Catholic Bishops Conference, with the pastoral plan of "COMMUNITY HELPING HUMANITY." It is effectively organizing small Christian communities (1,600 at present!), many of which now meet weekly in groups of 200 or more, then break into 15–20 sub-groups during the week. LUMKO also offers courses to Pastoral Animators who wish to learn how to train others in specific pastoral/catechetical skills and their underlying theological vision. LUMKO is doing nothing less than training people for a new creation, preparing blacks and whites to live together in a in a new society.

NEW NATION . . . is the national Catholic publication with a subscriber rate of 55,000 (5,000 street vendors). It is published weekly and not always a welcome sight to the government. When I was in Pretoria, South Africa, I was able to get the first issue after New Nation had been closed for 3 months by the government (the third closure in a year!). The editor had been in prison for over two years!

IMP ... founded by Gain Coulson in 1977, is the Interchurch Media Programme, whose purpose is to help those engaged in living out Christian values in Southern Africa today to communicate more effectively in spiritual, community, and educational development. It is a Christian experiment in the creative use of media for and by ordinary people. There is a charismatic aspect to IMP in the sense that both staff and director try to respond to needs of Christian communities with their particular personal gifts and insights, achieving something that is multi-dimensional in terms of technical skills integrated into a faith vision and a political conviction. This living, dynamic element has its source in the staff who try to make this "adventure IMP" a service and a commitment to the liberation in South Africa.

THE BLACK SASH ... is a movement of 20,000 middle class white women working for an end to apartheid and the dehumanizing system of South Africa. They make themselves available to advise blacks of their rights in such areas as retrenchments, dismissals, Workmen's Compensation, ID and citizenship, housing, divorce and imprisonment.

SOUTHERN AFRICA

Television is not a good way to reach people in many African countries, because:

1. they see TV as a top-down, state-owned, government-operated tool of oppression and propaganda;

2. they think (and they are correct) that video cameras are used by police to take pictures of people who create "unrest" or threaten the establishment — so they can retaliate later;

3. when they do watch any TV, they see it only as show biz entertainment.

Two more effective media for reaching people in Africa are:
MUSIC: especially sing-alongs in harmony
DANCE: especially sacred and cultural dance (e.g. a foot- stomping aerobics-like circle dance where different individuals go in the middle of the circle, set a rhythm and then lead a chant which is frequently improvised with a refrain sung by all — much more lyrical and melodic than "rap"—while the rest of the spectators/participants clap and stomp in time).

Interestingly, both music and dance are rhythmic, harmonic, spontaneous, freeing, circular, shared, refrained . . .

NEW NATION: some figures

- 72% of South Africa's population is Christian.

- The largest multi-racial church is the Catholic Church.

- In a survey, 31.4% of whites said they believed religious movements should take a stand against racial discrimination.

If you are neutral in situations of injustice, you have chosen the side of the oppressor. If an elephant has his foot on the tail of a mouse and you say that you are neutral, the mouse will not appreciate your neutrality. **Bishop Desmond Tutu**

Hiding Jesus

There are people after Jesus.
They've seen the signs.
Quick, let's hide him.
Let's think: carpenter
fisherman's friend
disturber
of religious comfort—
let's award him a degree in theology,
a purple cassock and
a position of respect.
They'll never think of looking here.
Let's think: his dialect may betray him,
His tongue
is of the masses
Let's teach him Latin
and seventeenth century English
they'll never think of listening in.
Let's think: humble,
man of sorrows,
nowhere
to lay his head
We'll build a house for him,
somewhere away from the poor.
We'll fit it with brass and silence
It's sure to throw them off.
There are people after Jesus.
Quick, let's hide him.

Steve Turner
(Courtesy of Salt)

At-ONE-MENT

Parable of Married Communication

When a man whose marriage was in trouble sought his advice, the Master said, "You must learn to listen to your wife." The man took this advice to heart and returned after a month to say that he had learned to listen to every word his wife was saying.

Said the Master with a smile, "Now go home and listen to every word she isn't saying."

WEST AFRICA

A **T A GLANCE**   **LIBERIA**
Population: *2,600,000*
Capital With Population: *Monrovia*
Language: *English, tribal dialects*
Literacy: *25%*
Faith Expression: *Traditional beliefs 70%,*
     Moslem 20%, Christian 10%
Currency Used: *U.S. dollar*

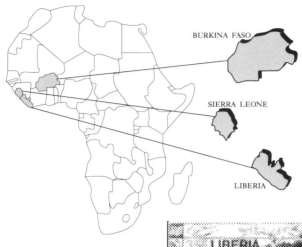

BURKINA FASO

SIERRA LEONE

LIBERIA

LIBERIA

Monrovia

POSTCARD
R E F L E C T I O N S

Liberia: land of freedom, established by President James Monroe (Monrovia) as the homeland in Africa for expatriate freed American slaves. . . so many signs of similarity . . . look-alike flags . . . and many cultural cross-overs (like Country and Western music and Paul Simon on the Catholic Radio Station . . .) still, unmistakably, inexpressibly Africa.

LIBERIA, HAVEN FOR ALL

Smiles to go

On the door of a hotel room:

If this is your first visit to our city, you are welcome to it.

Monrovia, LIBERIA

WEADE KOBBAH WUREH: dedicated wife, busy mother, news reporter, radio personality, station manager and diocesan director of communication—tough, loving, smiling, with high energy, balance and grace—a one-woman whirlwind in charge of ELCM (FM 97.8), the only Catholic radio station in all of Africa.

ARCHBISHOP MICHAEL FRANCIS: answers his own phone — and that tells you everything you need to know about him as a man and a bishop and a communicator!

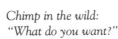

*Chimp in the wild:
"What do you want?"*

Well, here we are in the wild! Nothing quaint, picturesque . . . no missionary mystique. Just pouring rain, a muddy downtown jungle and the gridlock of human poverty . . . not to mention the political corruption and the hopelessness of a people who have learned to live with their problems instead of solving them. A different type of slavery. Communication here is shortwave radio, church here is long range heroism.

*Chimp in the wild:
"Peek-A-Boo"*

59

WEST AFRICA

A T A GLANCE   *SIERRA LEONE*
Population: 4,500,000
Capital With Population: Freetown 500,000
Language: English, local tribal languages
Literacy: 15%
Faith Expression: Animist 30%; Moslem 30%,
        Christian 10% and localreligions
Currency Used: Leone

PROFILES

Creative Communicators

**Freetown,
SIERRA LEONE**

FR. ED GRIMES:
hospitable, helpful and in charge of almost everything . . . you can hear the static and chatter of the open short-wave radio transmitter receiver that keeps this far-flung diocesan network together — like bustling cab drivers with their two-way radios! Most church communicating in West Africa is still via print media: such as Gambia's "Pastoral Institute Newsletter" and "The Sierra Leone Catholic Magazine."

FR. BRIAN STARKEN:
big, gentle, caring communicator who runs a spiritual-educational growth center up-country and uses AV media whenever and wherever possible.

SIERRA LEONE

Freetown

"I've been told I have a great face for radio," said one church executive after watching his TV news interview played back on videotape. For many church people around the world my three or five day communications workshop was the first time they had seen themselves on TV. For some, it was an unnerving experience. For others, it was a cause for pride and joy. One religious spokesperson in the South Pacific, after watching himself on TV for the first time, beamed: *"I like me. I am a gift from God. I like me in person—and on TV."* We should all be so blessed.

During the workshops, I emphasized to the bishops, religious superiors and church leaders that Christian communication is like parenting, preaching or teaching: what you ultimately communicate is you—your faith, your hope, your love. And the most effective medium for that spiritual communication is storytelling, as Jesus' parables continue to remind us 2,000 years later. So I encouraged the workshop participants to tell stories of faith. My favorites so far are the two parables on pages 62 and 63.

Former railway station built in 1898, Freetown

60

A T A GLANCE   *BURKINA FASO*
Population: 7,704,000
Capital With Population: Ouagadougou 400,000
Language: French, Sudanic tribal languages
Literacy: 8%
Faith Expression: Animist 65%, Moslem 25%,
Christian 10%
Currency Used: CFA Franc

CREATIVE
COMMUNICATING

IDEAS IN MEDIA MINISTRY

Ouagadougou

BURKINA FASO

OBSTACLES TO DEVELOPING CATHOLIC COMMUNICATIONS IN WEST AFRICA AND THROUGHOUT AFRICA AT LARGE*

- radio studios too small for proper recording and training and poorly set up; many broadcasts entirely produced in Church studio, with limitations

- productivity hampered by hot weather

- insufficient funds for new equipment; old equipment outdated

- not enough full-time personnel and inadequate salaries and subsidies

- dependence on state television studio, which is costly and often not accessible (Catholic communications comes last on priority list)

- lack of communication training opportunities and resources

- need for Catholic broadcasts translated in different national languages

- need for wider variety of programs

- need for airtime on commercial television and radio

- need for scholarships for training personnel

- need for on-going formation of those already involved in communications

- shortage of black talent for Catholic radio and TV programs

*Based on responses from Church communicators in Africa to a questionnaire sent by Fr. Roger Tessier in 1986 as part of an assessment of the apostolate of social communications in Africa.

WEST AFRICA

ELCM (FM 97.8)

Community Radio with the motto "Laus Tibi Christe" ("Praise you Jesus") and the slogan "We are the worthwhile spot on your radio."

The only Catholic Church owned and operated radio station broadcasting in Africa: on the air from 6:00 p.m. to midnight, Monday through Saturday, 9:00 a.m. to midnight on Sunday.

Progams include spiritual talks from Archbishop Fulton Sheen and Paulist Communications; educational programming on farming, science, language study, poetry, and health; religious shows including the Mass, rosary, charismatic renewal and bible study; regular news, editorials and lots of gospel music sprinkled throughout . . . a vital, audible evangelizing presence in the community!

As proof of ELCM's prophetic voice and value in the Liberian community, it was closed down last year by the government.

Parable of the "Wheat Seed"

One day a little seed buried in a field looked up and noticed a tall, elegant stalk of wheat growing nearby. The grain admired the wheat and wanted to be like him. "Excuse me," said the seed, "what must I do to become like you?"

"Nothing," answered the wheat, "only be yourself, buried in the earth—and God's tears in the rain and smile in the sun will give you new life and you will grow up to be just like me."

Later that day, a lovely lamb wandered into the field and began grazing near the stalk of wheat. The wheat gazed fondly at the fleecy white lamb: "Dear lamb, what must I do to become like you?"

"You have nothing to do," replied the lamb tenderly, "only to be yourself and let me eat you. Then you will become like me."

Later that same day, a man entered the field. The lamb was fascinated by the man and drew close with admiration. "What must I do to become like you?" The man answered, "Only be yourself and let me eat you—you will become like me."

Later, when the man asked, with longing and love, what he must do to become like God, God answered: "You must do nothing but be yourself and I will send my son to become like you, a man, the lamb of God, sacrificed for your sins, buried in the ground to rise up to new life. You have only to eat him in the wheat bread of communion and you will become one with God."

Parable of the African Lion

The second story of faith was told by a missionary who, on his arrival in darkest Africa, was surprised to find that God had already arrived—well ahead of the missionaries—and was wonderfully alive among the native people. Still, the missionary felt obliged to preach his Christian faith and testified as eloquently as possible in the local language to the God of Sacred Scripture.

After his service and sermon, the tribal chief approached the missionary and challenged him gently: "Reverend, when you speak of faith, you use words similar to those used to describe a white hunter killing a lion with a long-range rifle. There is little commitment or involvement. Only the eye in the gunsight and the finger on the trigger are engaged in the act.

"For us the act of faith is more like the action of the lion stalking its prey, following patiently, racing swiftly, pouncing mightily with its whole being, wrapping its strong legs and paws around its prey, clutching it to his body until he has taken its life and then devouring it, transforming it into himself. For us, the act of faith is total."

The missionary said he stood speechless, stunned by the simple eloquence and theological insight of this naked native who understood real faith so much better than any book or sermon. Just then, tears filled the missionary's eyes and he told me: "But the wise chief wasn't finished with me yet. He had one more lesson for the teacher to learn. He started to walk away and then came back to me and said, 'Reverend, for us faith is like the capture and kill of a powerful lion who puts his entire being into the act. Only in our faith, the lion is God.' "

I, too, was the temporary African missionary, traveling and teaching, but mostly learning in a land we call "the dark continent" but which long ago was enlightened by Christ. Here the Catholic faith grows deeper and faster than anywhere else. I learned from the world we dare to call the "Third World" as if it were in third place in some global economic race. In fact it may refer ironically to a third level—well above a first world, first level—closer to what really matters. Please pray for your African brothers and sisters and this temporary missionary and yourselves—that God will devour us all.

EAST AFRICA

A T A GLANCE KENYA
Population: 23,727,000
Capital with population: Nairobi 960,000
Language: Swahili, English
Literacy: 50%
Faith Expression: Protestant 38%,
   Roman Catholic 26%, Moslem 6% and others
Currency Used: Shilling
Average Salary: $60/month

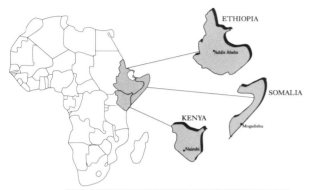

KENYA

POSTCARD
REFLECTIONS

In Nairobi, Kenya, during a 5-day media workshop for 15 national communication directors from 7 east African countries, I asked the participants for examples of inculturation in their area. Sr. Catherine of Ethiopia explained beautifully how "ashes" failed to symbolize repentance and renewal. Instead, for the Ethiopians, ashes were the sign of humiliation and degradation. So they simply changed the symbol from ashes to seeds: a powerful, meaningful image in Africa and an obvious sign of life, death, growth and Easter hope.

The first time I walked into an African church, I asked where the organ or piano was. The pastor replied patiently "We don't need those—we have these," and pointed to a set of conga drums. "Our people make the music."

Smiles to go

In an East African newspaper:

A new swimming pool is rapidly taking shape since the contractors have thrown in the bulk of their workers.

FR. PETER LWOMINDA: attractive, affable, gifted linguist, former Executive Secretary for Zambian Bishops' Conference, now Executive Secretary for AMECEA, consortium of seven countries of East Africa: Ethiopia, Kenya, Uganda, Tanzania, Sudan, Zambia, and Malawi.

FR. PAUL URIA: classy, kind, committed communicator and compassionate priest, Communications Coordinator for AMECEA, who understands that, in Africa's over 50 countries with some 7,000 distinct languages, communication involves much more than words — he is sensitive to Africa's deepest spiritual and cultural values: life, fecundity, ancestors ("the living dead"), the blood pact of brotherhood, kinship and medicine . . .

Masai warriors

"I HOPE YOUR COWS ARE WELL"

. . . The Masai greeting

Cows supply their life drink, SAROI, a mix of warm blood and fresh milk from the cow.

To the Masai, cows, grass and land are sacred: the land belongs to God — ENKAI — and cannot be "pierced" to cultivate or to bury the dead.

Masai girls

EAST AFRICA

AT A GLANCE   *ETHIOPIA*
Population: *47,709,000*
Capital With Population: *Addis Ababa 1,500,000*
Language: *Amharic, Tigre (Semitic languages),*
          Galla (Hamitic), Arabic, others
Literacy: *18%*
Faith Expression: *Orthodox Christian 40%, Moslem 40%*
Currency Used: *Birr*

PROFILES
Creative Communicators

SR. CATHERINE GAYNOR:
communications director for Ethiopia and marvelous media missionary who knows how to inculturate communication: by changing "bread" to "food" e.g. "Our Father . . . give us this day our daily food" (in areas where there is no flour or wheat or bread) or by exchanging the "ashes" of Ash Wednesday (which for many were a sign of humiliation and disrespect) for "seeds" (which serve as signs of Easter hope: life, death and resurrection) or by incorporating traditional African forgiveness rites: giving the gift of beer and goats to the offended tribe, or placing your hand on the shoulder of the wronged person as you ask forgiveness, or breaking a twig to symbolize that the offense is forgiven and forgotten.

FR. LUCAS MASSAWE:
tall, humorous, fun, friendly communications director for Dar Es Salaam, Tanzania, where the pilgrim people, the living church, think of themselves as the "5th Gospel" and find simple earthy ways to communicate that Good News!

ETHIOPIA

•Addis Ababa

KENYA

Black Jesus

Jesus was Italian. Or was He French? Or Palestinian? In Africa I have met a black Jesus. The Son of God, Jesus of Nazareth, hanging on the cross, has African hair, skin, nose and lips. The Madonna pictured nursing the baby Jesus at her abundant black breasts wears the features and tribal beauty marks of a typical African mother nursing on a crowded Nairobi bus today. It shocks us Westerners only because most of the holy cards we grew up with were painted by Europeans.

Theologically, this is called incarnation. Jesus of Nazareth became fully human at a particular time and place in history; he belonged to a particular people, culture, religion.

Sociologically, this is called inculturation: making Jesus present and real in Africa today.

"If Christianity's claim to be universal is to be believed, then it is not Africa that must be Christianized but Christianity that must be Africanized." . . . Bishop Peter Sarpong of Ghana

A T A GLANCE   SOMALIA
Population: 8,552,000
Capital With Population: Mogadishu 710,000
Language: Somalia, Arabic
Literacy: 40%
Faith Expression: Sunni Moslem 99%
Currency Used: Shilling

SOMALIA

•Mogadishu

PROFILES

Creative Communicators

DR. DEOGRATIAS, KIKAWA & SR. GERMINA KENEEMA: a smiling, efficient, talented team of religious videographers and communicators in Uganda who share the spotlight with others.

FR. DICK QUINN, M.M: generous, gifted, most respected, one of the "grandfathers" of the contemporary Catholic media ministry in Africa . . . trains and collaborates with young talent to use his 3 video cameras to make documentaries and help others tell their story . . . allowed us to use his equipment for our 5-full-day workshop in Nairobi for the national communication directors from the seven East African (AMECEA) countries.

FR. ROGER TESSIER: Executive Secretary of CEPACS, extremely well read and well organized researcher and one of the most insightful communication specialists in Africa (indeed in the world!) who knows the scene and the needs and the players — works tirelessly to facilitate Good News communication. . . and has produced some of the best studies of Catholic Communications in Africa.

SWAHILI JINGLE

Jambo, Jambo sana (hello, hello a lot)
Habari gani (how are you?)
Mzuri sana (very well)
Wageni mwakaribishwa (visit us—you are welcome)
Hapa Kenya (here in Kenya)
Hakuna matata (no problem)

PRAYER FOR TOURISTS

Dear God, look down on us your humble tourists, who are doomed to travel this earth, taking photographs, sending postcards, shopping for souvenirs and walking around in drip-dry underwear.

Give us this day divine guidance in the selection of our hotels and lodges, that we may find our reservations honored, our rooms made up and hot water running from the taps.

We pray that the telephones work, and the operators answer and speak our language.

Lead us, dear Lord, to good, inexpensive restaurants where the food is superb, the waiters friendly and the wine included in the price.

Give us the wisdom to tip correctly in currencies we do not understand. Forgive us for undertipping out of ignorance and overtipping out of fear. Make the people love us for what we are, and not for what we can contribute to their wordly goods.

Grant us the endurance to visit the lodges and game reserves listed as "musts" in the guidebooks.

And if perchance we skip an important game ride to take a nap after lunch, have mercy on us, for our flesh is weak.

EAST AFRICA

Much of Africa does not have bread, so often the Our Father is changed to "Give us this day our daily food."

When I visited the Turkana tribe of northwest Kenya, I went from village hut to campfire, giving God's blessing to the people until a wise guide informed me: "Father, when you raise your hand in blessing like that, the children think you are going to hit them."

Masai tribesmen

Another radical difference between Africa and America is the sense of time. In the U.S. Sunday Mass lasts 55 minutes—give or take a second collection, special announcements or a runaway homily. Africans don't live in clock time as we do; they create time; they do something until it's done. Their liturgies last two to three hours. They celebrate in grand style until it's done. Whether waiting for a bus, celebrating their faith or visiting a friend—they do it calmly and completely and then, like the seasons, move patiently onto the next.

Africa is twice as big as the United States: 555 million people in more than 50 nations, speaking more than 7,000 distinct languages. That makes communicating and inculturating difficult. Cardinal Ottunga of Nairobi, during a private visit, said, "Inculturation is the Church's challenge in Africa today, and it's working—but slowly." One of the biggest hurdles is habit: older Africans are so accustomed to a white European Jesus, Italian Holy Family and organ music that they resist inculturation and are uncomfortable with clapping, dancing and drums in church.

One African man described religion as "the skin that you carry along with you wherever you are, not like the cloth that you wear now and discard later." God is described concretely as "Source of all Life," "Eternal Chief," "Nursing Mother" and "Piler of Rocks into Towering Mountains." Sin is described as "the insect that sticks into our skin and sucks our lifeblood." In the old days, the sinner had to make reparation to the whole tribe—there was an African earth wisdom that sin somehow hurt the entire family and community.

Today some break twigs to symbolize forgiveness—a break with the past—or they reverently place a hand on the left shoulder of the other person as a sign of total forgiveness. Once done, the incident can never be recalled by the person who forgives (an "Africanization" that would benefit Christians everywhere).

I have vivid recollection of celebrating Mass with my African brothers and sisters, rhythmically tapping and clapping, swaying and praying, wondering if I don't have a little African blood deep in me—and wondering if we'll ever have an American Jesus.

EAST AFRICA

AMECEA Social Communications Department

The **Association of Member Episcopal Conferences in East Africa** maintains a communications secretary (Fr. Paul Uria) and an office in Nairobi. This central office animates and develops religious communications projects for the whole seven country region, obtains financial grants and scholarships, handles information and press office duties including a quarterly newsletter, and conducts training workshops for its member nations in mass media and group media.

CREATIVE
COMMUNICATING

SWAHILI PROVERBS

"When the elephants fight, the grass gets hurt."

"I pointed out to you the moon and all you saw was my finger."

"The greatest good we can do for others is not just to share our riches with them but to reveal their riches to themselves."

"Patience is the key to tranquility."

"Would you give food to your children that you won't eat yourself?" (Re: importance of living faith before baptizing child.)

"The water in a coconut shell is like an ocean to an ant."

"Karibu Chakula" ("Welcome to the food")

"A visitor is a guest for two days: on the third day give the person a hoe."

"A slow rain bears the most fruit."

"Hurry, hurry has no blessing."

"Chip, chip finishes the log."

"You're not a white man — you're our father."

"Education is an ocean."

"To dig is weariness: to reap is joy."

"To marry off your son is to swallow a stone."

"A promise is a debt."

When the elephants fight, the grass gets hurt.

THE PARABLE OF THE SEEDS

A woman dreamt she walked into a brand new shop in the marketplace and, to her surprise, found God behind the counter.

"What do you sell here?" she asked.

"Everything your heart desires," said God.

Hardly daring to believe what she was hearing, the woman decided to ask for the best things a human being could wish for.

"I want peace of mind and love and happiness and wisdom and freedom from fear," she said. Then as an afterthought she added, "Not just for me. For everyone on earth."

God smiled. "I think you've got me wrong, my dear," he said.

"We don't sell fruits here. ONLY SEEDS."

ASIA

KOREA

A T A GLANCE   **SOUTH KOREA**

Population: 39,950,000
Capital With Population: Seoul 9,600,000
Language: Korean
Literacy: 92%
Faith Expression: Buddhist, Confucianist, Christian
Currency Used: Won
Cities I visited: Seoul

Downtown Seoul – Southgate

POSTCARD REFLECTIONS

Ahn Yong Ha Say Yo= GREETINGS!
literally: "stay in peace!"
(everyday "hello" in Korean)

Met with the station coordinators MBC-KBS (Korea) who provided the universal feed for the Olympics in '88. It was just like a Papal visit – only less expensive.

Someone said this news article means . . .

"Fr. Miles gives media workshop to Korean Cardinal, Bishops, and Priests."

Don't believe it!

There are no coincidences. . .

While in Seoul, Korea I pick up the International Herald Tribune and what is my favorite American satirist, Gary Trudeau, talking about? You guessed it .

INTERNATIONAL HERALD TRIBUNE WEDNESDAY, AUGUST 24, 1988

DOONESBURY

PROFILES
Creative Communicators

CARDINAL STEPHEN KIM: possible candidate for the next pope, commented on the phenomenal growth rate of the Catholic Church in Korea: "the challenge is that the thousands of new converts coming in the front door of the church are walking out the back door two years later. The solution is two-fold: small Christian communities and holiness—we must organize more and better SCC's where Catholics feel they belong, are greeted by name and are missed if they don't come; but the most important deterent to the drop-out of our people is the holiness of our clergy and religious and lay leaders!"

PROFESSOR PAUL CHOI: warm, witty, well versed University media teacher and active as an advisor/consultant to the Catholic Church in Korea and all of Asia—particularly in his role as president of UNDA-OCIC Korea, a group of 300 Catholic lay professionals working in the broadcast industry in Seoul who meet monthly, support one another creatively and spiritually, and work to incorporate Christian themes and truths in their work.

KOREA

FR. RAY SULLIVAN:
host with the most, one of the Maryknoll's finest–along with Fr. Mike Duggan and others — and Maryknoll missionaries are consistently among the finest in the world—recently celebrated his 61st birthday so he is revered as an elder deserving of special respect (most countries in the world give added reverence and respect to folks as they grow older. How did the U.S. tragically reverse this: giving progressively less respect until our elderly reach an arbitrary age like 65 or 75 and can be dismissed, or worse, forgotten all together?). Fr. Ray uses popular music–cassettes, pop tunes, musicals, etc. to reach the masses (especially the youthful) and communicate gospel values.

FR. WAYNE SCHMIDT:
one of those tall aggressive, assertive "John Wayne Type A's" who won't take "no" for an answer–only "yes, sir!" and who drove to Seoul to bring me up the "38th parallel" to give a "day of recollection" to the U.S. Military Chaplains in Korea and afterward tape several short featurette radio shows à la "Good Morning, Korea!" for the American Forces Radio station in Korea. We taped little "thoughts for the day".

CREATIVE
COMMUNICATING

IDEAS IN MEDIA MINISTRY

Perfect Pastor and No Excuse Sunday are two of the spots I recorded for American Forces Radio in Korea:

PERFECT PASTOR

Results of a computerized survey indicate that the perfect pastor preaches exactly 15 minutes. He condemns sin, but never upsets anyone. He works from 8 a.m. 'til midnight and is also the janitor. He makes $60 a week, wears good clothes, buys good books, drives a good car, and gives about $50 a week to the poor.

He is twenty-eight years old and has been preaching for thirty years. He is wonderfully gentle and handsome. He has a burning desire to work with teenagers and spends all his time with senior citizens.

The perfect pastor smiles all the time with a straight face because he has a sense of humor that keeps him seriously dedicated to his work. He makes 15 calls a day on parish families, shut-ins and hospitalized; spends all his time evangelizing the un-churched and is always in his office when needed.

If your pastor does not measure up, simply send this letter to six other parishes that are tired of their pastor, too. Then bundle up your pastor and send him to the church at the top of the list. In one year, you will receive 1,643 pastors – and one of them should be perfect.

Warning: keep this letter going. One parish broke the chain and got its old pastor back in less than three months.

NO EXCUSE SUNDAY

To make it possible for everyone to attend church next Sunday, we are going to have a special "No Excuse Sunday."

Cots will be placed in the vestibule for those who say, "Sunday is my only day to sleep." We will have steel helmets for those who say, "The roof would cave in if I ever came back to church." Blankets will be furnished for those who think the church is too cold; fans will be provided for those who say it's too hot.

We will have hearing aids for those who say the pastor speaks too softly, and cotton for those who say he preaches too loudly. Score cards will be available for those who like to list all the hypocrites.

A few floating unattached relatives will be in attendance for those who like to visit on Sundays. One entire section will be landscaped with real shrubbery and astro turf for those who find God in nature on Sunday mornings.

Finally, the sanctuary will be decorated with both Christmas poinsettias and Easter lilies for those who have never seen the church without them.

It's No Excuse Sunday!
See you in church!

PROFILES
Creative Communicators

FR. PAUL OH:
master organizer, understands as few church leaders do, the importance of planning. Completed his theological studies in Rome, so much of our dialog was in Italian with Father Paul translating my comments into Korean (it's a small "global village!"). The Korean clergy have a voracious appetite for data, information, factual knowledge, and they are beginning to see that "communication," like "faith," is also a verb: not just things you write and say, but actions you do. They are building studios to create video and audio programs and they are conducting practical seminars to enable their preachers and teachers to perfect their art through on-camera exercises.

PARABLE OF SELF-KNOWLEDGE

The Master was an advocate both of Learning and of Wisdom.

"Learning," he said when asked, "is gotten by reading books or listening to lectures."

"And Wisdom?"

"By reading the book that is you."

He added as an afterthought: "Not an easy task at all, for every minute of the day brings a new edition of the book!"

JAPAN

AT A GLANCE   JAPAN
Population: 123,231,000
Capital With Population: Tokyo
  8,150,000
Language: Japanese
Literacy: 99%
Faith Expression: Buddhist, Shinto,
  Roman Catholic

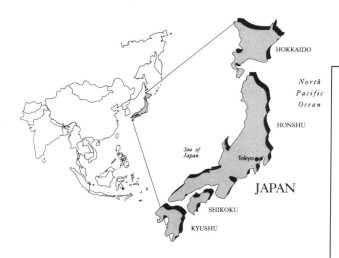

HOKKAIDO

North
Pacific
Ocean

HONSHU

Sea of
Japan

Tokyo

JAPAN

SHIKOKU

KYUSHU

Japan is winning the industrial race—but at a terrible cost (not just "yen") to their traditional cultural and family values: they are working 12–14 hours 6 days a week on the edge of burnout. A young father who sees his new son 2–3 hours a week, Sunday afternoon, explained to me, "If I don't take my office staff out for sushi and beer every evening from 7–10 p.m., the office spirit will go down and so will our productivity!" Every American should be required to visit Tokyo for one week: to see where we are headed if we do not stop and ask ourselves as a society: "What really matters in this life? What do we really want?"

I think I've found my sport. It's this—or go on a diet!...
                    Fat chance.

POSTCARD
REFLECTIONS

The ritual, ancient Sumo wrestling, Japan's national sport.

SMILES to go

In an advertisement by a dentist:

Teeth extracted by the latest Methodists.

We took the world's fastest "Bullet Train," shown here near snow-capped Mount Fuji, to a retreat center in the north for a workshop with Japan's religious film makers and videographers....

Time and Space...Africans have a different sense of time. They don't ask as we do at day's end, "How much did I accomplish today?" but rather, "How happy was I?"

Asians have a different sense of space. Homes, schools, shops, offices are all built to a more human scale: manageable, personal, even intimate.

...Too intimate if you ride the morning trains and subways around Tokyo where "packers" literally cram people into the cars like sushi in a can of soy sauce. One Japanese nun said it made her feel closer to God's people, the Body of Christ.

PROFILES

Creative Communicators

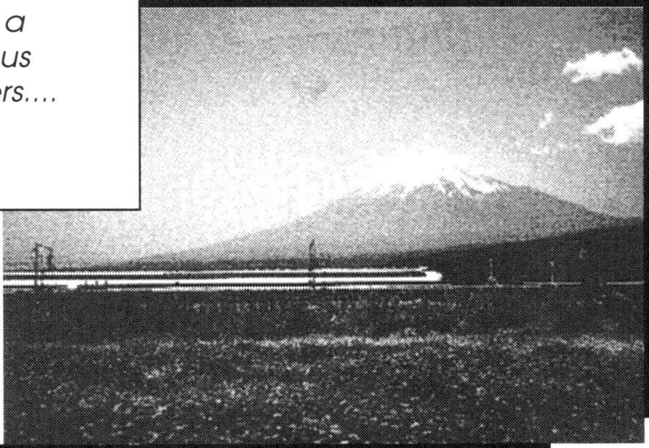

FR. JOSE M. DE VERA, S.J: director of Sophia University's Television Center, top Jesuit University in Tokyo, one of the great grand gentlemen of international religious communications, teaches "Mass Media and Human Behavior" and "TV Production," serves as Bureau Chief for UCAN News in Japan, gives lectures worldwide, publishes frequently and most interestingly teaches a Bible course for the hundreds of non-Christian Japanese couples who are fascinated by our Catholic churches and our wedding ritual, but do not have the grace gift of faith!—a Catholic priest will preside at the "church" wedding—but only after 6 months of weekly meetings and study of the Bible, the Church and the faith (we should be so blessed with our own Catholic couples!): the priests see this as a creative form of evangelization outreach to the 99% of the Japanese population which is non-Christian.

I like taking my shoes off before entering a living space (sacred space): liberated feet feel more of the earth and creation.

JAPAN

PROFILES
Creative Communicators

SR. MARY JOSEPH SHOKO SHIRAI, FSP:
non-stop energy and enthusiasm, kindness and professionalism, "Shoko," as she is known to her many friends worldwide, will show you her slide library, one of the best organized and most comprehensive in the world and will show you her Japanese culture by giving you a tour of Tokyo's department stores which reveal the interests, lifestyle and values of her country. A film and video producer, Sr. Shoko belongs to the Sisters of St. Paul, who operate shops with Catholic books and religious articles as their form of Pauline evangelization—a particularly powerful presence in non-Christian countries!

FR. MARIO BIANCHIN, FR. ROLAND JOLICOEUR, FR. SABURO T. MATSUMOTO (Director of Communications for the Bishops' Conference) and FR. PETER J. IWAHASHI (Secretary General of the Bishops' Conference):
are outstanding examples of other church leaders who understand the importance of a Catholic Mass and mini-media ministry in Japan. Fr. Mario Bianchin, for example, uses video productions as an integral part of his missionary endeavor in Japan—he calls them **The Pilgrimage.**

CREATIVE COMMUNICATING

IDEAS IN MEDIA MINISTRY

Daughters of St. Paul

In 1989 the Daughters of St. Paul in Tokyo produced 3 video programs, 5 CD titles, 10 audio cassettes—and created 80 3–4 minute recorded talks for their call-in telephone information ministry. (Why are so few Catholic communicators—e.g. France, India, Japan—using the telephone creatively for evangelization?) They supplied 70 film rentals, 6 film forums and 30 seminars.

Junrei: Chisai Mono No Inori
or
The Pilgrimage: The Prayer of Little Ones

The first video documentary treated the whole area of "prayer" in a way that the Japanese could understand.

Fr. Mario is now completing "The Pilgrimage: The Prayer of the Little Ones," a documentary on a pilgrimage to Assisi, Rome, The Holy Land, and Lourdes by a group of people with handicaps. As he explains: "The background is the event and teaching of Christ, the foreground is the people's own voyage of the heart and the invitation to put ourselves in the same spirit which makes us 'small' like the little children of the Gospel to whom the Kingdom of God belongs."

Film and Video

Japan, second to the United Kingdom, imports $100 million worth of U.S. films. In 1988 the Japanese watched 700 million films on video cassette.

Participants in Japan's O.C.I.C. Media Workshop, Tokyo, August 30, 1988. Sr. Shoke is second from right in back row, Fr. Mario is far left, Fr. Roland third from left, Fr. Jose fourth from left next to Miles.

FR. CHARLES BURAUS, FR. ROBERT REILEY, FR. EMILE DUMAS, and BROTHER RAY TETRAULT:
are Maryknoll missionaries who exemplify Maryknoll's commitment to service and at the same time, manage to provide a kind of American home-away-from-home where peanut butter cookies and milk comfort the frenzied tourist. One block from the Maryknoll House and another block from Sophia University is a nondescript exclusive restaurant frequented by chauffeur-driven Japanese executives: the "fixed price" for a simple lunch or supper is $1,400.00 U.S. (That is not a typographical error—it's another kind of error!)

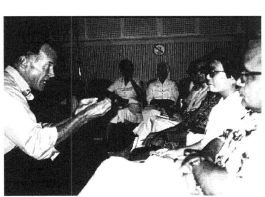

With a lot of help from several translators, communication tips are shared.

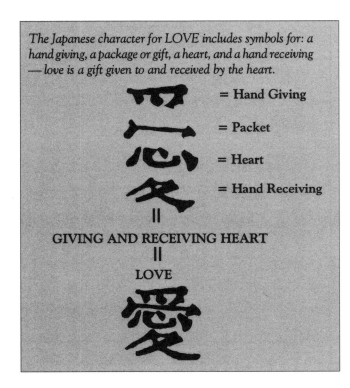

The Japanese character for LOVE includes symbols for: a hand giving, a package or gift, a heart, and a hand receiving — love is a gift given to and received by the heart.

= Hand Giving

= Packet

= Heart

= Hand Receiving

||

GIVING AND RECEIVING HEART

||

LOVE

PARABLE OF LOVE

"What is love?"
"The total absence of fear," said the Master.
"What is it we fear?"
"Love," said the Master.

TAIWAN

A T A GLANCE   TAIWAN

Population: 20,283,000
Capital with Population: Taipei 2,575,000
Language: Mandarin Chinese, Taiwan
Literacy: 90%
Faith expression: Confucianist, Buddhist, Taoist
Currency used: New Taiwan Dollar
Cities Visited: Taipei

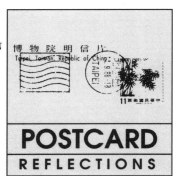

POSTCARD
REFLECTIONS

Bird's eye view of the National Palace Museum.

Spent an afternoon at the lovely, well appointed Nation's Museum. Serene, informative, air-conditioned. The rest of Taipei is frantic, hectic, crowded, busy, noisy, dusty—the most bodies per square centimeter (except for Bangladesh) in the world!

This is one of six panels displayed in the museum, which together represent Giuseppe Castiglione's famous long handscroll.

Giuseppe Castiglione (1688–1766) entered the Society of Jesus (The Jesuits) in 1707 at the age of 19 and became a Jesuit brother. He arrived in the Far East (China) in 1715. He studied Chinese and acclimatized himself to the culture as a good missionary would. He served the Emperors and the Kingdom of God as a communicator, as an artist—using his art and contacts to open China to other Christian missionaries. He spent the next 52 years in China serving the Inner Court of three Emperors:

K'Ang-Hsi (1662-1722)
Yung-Cheng (1723-1735)
Ch'ien-Lung (1736-1796)

The panels contain one hundred horses and show his western sense of perspective with oriental shadows and source of light. His technical virtuosity, meticulous brush work, opulent coloring, well suited Imperial tastes (refined and richly elegant) and (I must say) my own as well....especially since I stayed with the Jesuits in Taipei!

Outside a tailor shop

Ladies may have a fit upstairs.

Smiles to go

KOREAN WC

These are the visuals (hand-drawn) to accompany a 60-sec. spot by one of my Korean participants at the Kuangchi Workshop in Taiwan.

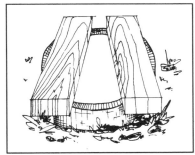

The story concerns a farmer who visits the outhouse after supper one night and falls asleep reading....

Fortunately, his elbows catch the sides and prevent his falling into the deep, dark, dank, dangerous You-Know-What (pit, of course!)...

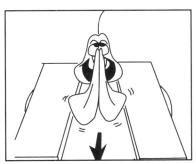

He is so grateful, he clasps his hands in prayer to God —

Of course, you know, and the visuals tell, the rest of the story with the unhappy ending.

TAIWAN

IDEAS IN MEDIA MINISTRY

CREATIVE COMMUNICATING

PROFILES
Creative Communicators

"TITA":
Kuangchi's secretary, coordinator, chief minister of hospitality, surrogate mom. Successful communication centers worldwide always seem to possess at least two key leaders: a head and a heart—a charismatic director who articulates a creative vision, and a healer-humanizer-"hoper" who holds hands and heads and everyone together. "Momma Tita" is Kuangchi's heart.

BISHOP PAUL CHAN, S.J:
one of a handful of Catholic bishops worldwide who truly understand the role and value of the mass media in the work of the Church. Bishop Paul mixes Jesuit brilliance with pastoral compassion as Bishop of Hualien, Taiwan, and adds a heavy dose of personal charm and awareness—all of which make him a superb spokesman and gifted communicator.

KPS

KUANGCHI PROGRAM SERVICE . . . is the largest, most productive TV, film, AV and radio production center run by the Catholic Church today. It is a non-profit organization founded by California Jesuits in 1958 to produce educational, recreational and religious programming. With a potential audience of 20 million, it produces 600 Chinese TV programs per year, broadcast daily throughout Taiwan. As a thorough-going program/production creative service center for the Church, it supports itself largely by producing public service and community affairs shows, videos and documentaries, frequently winning Taiwan's "Oscar" and "Emmy" awards for top productions. It earns its claim as "an audio-visual city of LIGHT and INSPIRATION at the service of Chinese communities throughout the world."

光 *KUANG*

LIGHT

啓 *CHI*

INSPIRATION

Participants in Kuangchi Program service video workshop learn how to create "commercial spots" with spiritual values.

"Beyond the Killing Fields"

One of the most powerful and effective documentaries I saw was Fr. Jerry Martinson and Kuangchi Program Service's "Beyond The Killing Fields" on the Cambodian refugees. Several video versions of the moving 45 minute documentary were distributed: raising much money, many awards and, most valuable, the consciousness (and consciences) of people worldwide and especially in Taiwan where it was broadcast in segments for several weeks.

production still

PARABLE FOR SINNERS

One of the disconcerting and delightful teachings of the Master was: "God is closer to sinners than to saints."

This is how he explained it: "God in heaven holds each person by a string. When you sin, you cut the string. Then God ties it up again, making a knot and thereby bringing you a little closer to Him. Again and again your sins cut the string and with each further knot God keeps drawing you closer and closer."

Dedicated to the tenderloin or soft sinful underbelly in every human city . . .

HONG KONG

GOD'S GRANDEUR
Gerard Manley Hopkins' poem set to images of Hong Kong

The world is charged with the grandeur of God.

It will flame out, like shining from shook foil;

It gathers to a greatness, like the ooze of oil crushed.

Why do men then now not reck his rod?

Generations have trod, have trod, have trod;

And all is seared with trade; bleared, smeared with toil;

And wears man's smudge and shares man's smell:

HONG KONG 香港

The soil is bare now, nor can foot feel, being shod.

HONG KONG 香港

And for all this, nature is never spent; there lives the dearest freshness deep down things;

HONG KONG 香港

And though the last lights off the black West went

HONG KONG 香港

Oh, morning, at the brown brink eastward, springs

HONG KONG 香港

Because the Holy Ghost over the bent World broods with warm breast and with ah! bright wings.

HONG KONG 香港

87

HONG KONG

FR. LOUIS HA:
consummate professional and one of the most pastoral church communicators in the world, he is director of the Hong Kong Catholic Communications Office and Editor of the diocesan newspaper **Kung Kao Bo**, and he emphasizes media education: "We now place considerable stress on media education," he says. "We believe there is a great need to teach people (children, parents and university students) to understand the function and operations of the different media. People must know how to distinguish the contents of the message. We want to train them to be a very active audience—and not just to receive everything in a passive way from the media." Fr. Ha has a good attitude about being a church spokesman: "This is an important and sensitive part of my job," he says. "I feel that I am a bridge, a go-between. I have to tell the truth; I cannot sacrifice my honesty in order to make the Church look good. At the same time, however, I cannot betray the Church because I am an officer of the Church." He is also a member of the Basic Law Consultation Committee and vitally concerned about the freedom and fate of Hong Kong when it is incorporated into Mainland China.

CARDINAL JOHN WU:
young, strong, affable, hospitable, with Canon Law precision and diplomatic awareness. Some suggest he will provide the ecclesiastical bridge between the Vatican and the Patriotic Catholic Church of Mainland China when Hong Kong is incorporated in 1997.

CREATIVE COMMUNICATING

Teachers and Department Heads enjoy playback and evaluation of their practice on camera news interviews.

IDEAS IN MEDIA MINISTRY

CATHOLIC SOCIAL COMMUNICATIONS

The Catholic Social Communications office offers some special services:

1 Media Education: especially for High School and College teachers, religious educators, and parish lay leaders who can help others learn how to live in our media culture with discretion, and to become critical consumers of communication.

2 Clippings Agency: the service has 150 subscribers, including secondary and tertiary institutions, journalists, university lecturers, Legislative Council and District Board members, and researchers in the business sector.

3 Training Workshops: for creative writers in television, film, and radio script-writing. The trainees are then helped to make the right connections so that their scripts can be produced!

In a dry cleaner's:

Drop your trousers here for best results.

The old and the new . . .

PARABLE OF GOD'S PRESENCE

"How does one seek union with God?"

"The harder you seek, the more distance you create between Him and you."

"So what does one do about the distance?"

"Understand that it isn't there."

"Does that mean that God and I are one?"

"Not one. Not two."

"How is that possible?"

"The sun and its light, the ocean and the wave, the singer and his song—not one, not two."

MACAU

A T A GLANCE   MACAU

Population: 450,000
Capital: Macau: 30,000
Language: Chinese, Portuguese
Currency: Pataca
Literacy: 99%

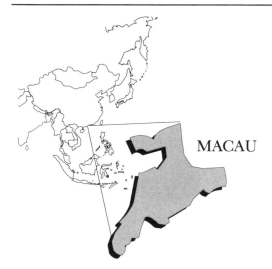

MACAU

Only the front door remains–but this St. Paul's facade is the symbol of Macau, here off the southern tip of China.

MANGO MOUSSE

macau

Forgive me for neglecting the culinary dimension & reports:

8 mangos,
350 grs. fresh cream,
8 soup spoons sugar,
juice of 2 oranges and 1 lemon,
1 1/2 packets plain jello and
1 liqueur glass of cointreau—equivalent in calories to jogging the island of Macau 200 times.

POSTCARD
REFLECTIONS

Smiles to go

In a hotel lobby:

The lift is being fixed for the next day. During that time we regret that you will be unbearable.

This is such a lovely little island. Country all green and growing and bathed in rain the week I was there.

Some weeks it's easier to leave a country than others — some places are easier to leave — this one is not easy!

91

MACAU

SR. MARIA PIA CANTIERI, D.S.P: powerful executive woman religious, in the tradition of a Mother Teresa of the Missionaries of Charity or Mother Angelica of the External World Network, who oversees and energizes a vast media ministry which includes radio and TV studios, daily broadcasts, and one of the biggest, busiest commercial theatres in Macau–the profits help subsidize the rest of the operation.

FR. AMERICO CASADO: kind, thoughtful, smiling Portuguese missionary who writes, produces and hosts most of the Portuguese language programming on Radio Macau (for a country that used to be a Portuguese territory) and complements "Madre Pia" in the spiritual leadership of this ambitious apostolate.

TERESINHA KOK: young, intelligent, lovely woman dedicated to religious communications, typifies the youthful crew of apostles who make "Centro Catolico" work so well: Francisco, Richard, Paulus, Michael, Betty, Iona, Ana, Agnes, Cheong, Luis and others.

UNDA-OCIC Asia Workshop September 25 - October 2, 1988

72 participants from 16 Asian countries

Participants in media workshop learning some do's and don'ts for press conferences and panel presentations.

CREATIVE
COMMUNICATING

IDEAS IN MEDIA MINISTRY

Diocesan Social Communications Center

The most comprehensive Catholic Communications Apostolate in the world:

RADIO: *programs in Chinese and Portuguese and training courses*

VIDEO: *production and recording center and "Salom Video Club"*

FILM: *major commercial theatre showing daily first-run features (which finances much of the communications apostolate) also cinema library, cultural center and classification committee*

ARTS-CULTURE: *activities, training, contests and festivals*

GROUP MEDIA: *cassettes, sound-slide, 16 mm and super-8 films, video*

PRESS & PUBLICITY: *St. Polycarp Library, St. Paul Bookstore, publication of articles, posters and parish bulletins*

Parable of the Mango

It was time for the monsoon rains to begin and a very old man was digging holes in his garden.
"What are you doing?" his neighbour asked.
"Planting mango trees," was the reply.
"Do you expect to eat mangoes from those trees?"
"No. I won't live long enough for that. But others will. It occurred to me the other day that all my life I have enjoyed mangoes planted by other people. This is my way of showing them my gratitude."

Have you planted a mango tree today?

CHINA

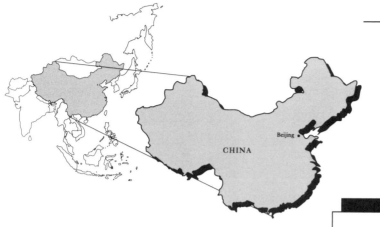

CHINA
Beijing

AT A GLANCE   **CHINA**

Population: *1,008,175,000*
Capital With Population: *Beijing 5,550,000*
Language: *Mandarin Chinese (official), Shanghai-, Canton-, Hakka-dialects, Tibetan, Vigus, Turkic*
Faith Expression: *Officially Atheist, Confucianist, Buddhist, Taoist*
Currency Used: *Yuan*
Cities I Visited: *Beijing*

PAR AVION

POSTCARD
REFLECTIONS

Sitting here in the Garden of the Forbidden City looking for the forbidden fruit. It was built in 1406: 9,000 rooms and 720,000 sq. meters, with 10 meter high walls and 52 meter wide moats; the Imperial Palace for Ming and Qing Dynasties (27 emperors, if I remember the tour guide). Oh, what these emperors could have done with money!

Law limits Chinese families to one child—they love children and hate the law and worry about a generation of spoiled only-children.

Beijing: City of more than 5 million people and almost 6 million bicycles (and several camels) and The Great Wall of China, the only thing on planet earth visible from the moon. 2,500 miles long, several stories high, two chariots wide, begun 2,000 years before Christ (B.C.): built to keep foreigners out, now brings them in! It's a wonderful wonder!

Smiles to go

Two signs in a shop entrance:

"English well talking"

"Here speeching American."

REV. THOMAS LIU:
gentle, concerned, humble rector of Immaculate Conception Cathedral in central Beijing who communicates from his heart—with the help of Mrs. Teresa Ying Muhlan and a thick dictionary—his deep desire for reunion with the Roman Catholic Church and his constant preoccupation that the Chinese government return some of the churches and schools which were confiscated to serve as factories.

BISHOP MICHAEL FU:
careful, earnest Bishop of Beijing trying to rebuild the Catholic Church in China—and the bridges to Rome.

FROM CHINA WITH LOVE

Someone, not Confucius, said that the Japanese prepare food for the eye, the Koreans for the body, and the Chinese for the guest. They made me their guest and revealed a little of their Asian grace and mystery. The Chinese are 25 percent of the world's population, working 7 percent of the earth's arable land: over one billion bicyclists in blue and gray, pumping hard but not yet happy.

PETITE HISTOIRE OF MODERN CHINA

1949	*Founding of Peoples' Republic of China by Mao and Communists (China now 3% Communist)*
1959	*China Catholic Patriotic Association breaks with Vatican*
1966–1976	*"Cultural Revolution"—Senile Mao eliminates intellectuals and threats*
1978	*"Open Door Policy"—4 modernizations.*

Land of 1.2 billion—1/4 world's pop (with 7% of world's arable land)

CHINA

CREATIVE
COMMUNICATING

IDEAS IN MEDIA MINISTRY

Catholic China

In the back of the peeled wooden Immaculate Conception Cathedral, I waited next to the chipped plaster imitations of the grotto of Lourdes and watched a devotional funeral service straight from my 1950 altar boy days at St. Catherine's in Burlingame. After Mass, 32 year old Fr. Thomas arrived with a military haircut and a heavy, high-collared black woolen suit that could have been issued by the costume department for "Going My Way."

Fr. Thomas welcomed me to his dank sitting room and, with the help of a little Latin and a big Chinese-English dictionary, told me of his people and parish—3 Masses a day, 2000 parishioners on Sunday, 300 adult baptisms a year—and of his hopes: to get back some of the Church's properties the government confiscated for factories during the "cultural revolution" and turn them into schools and senior citizen homes. He gave me a book and holy cards from his poverty and from his heart.

I asked when we would be part of the same Church and family again. He said, "We want to very much. We are waiting." He had tears in his eyes. We hugged good-bye at the door—and then at the gate and then at the taxi. The Chinese don't normally hug a lot. All we could share this visit was bread and tea. But Easter is coming to China.

The Church in China is reawakening. There are 4 Catholic parishes in Beijing and 6 more in the suburbs, 18 diocesan priests, 50 seminarians and 12 novices in the convent. I had an appointment with Beijing Bishop Michael Fu, one of 70 bishops in China now. Only three of the bishops go back 30 years to when the Chinese government decided Rome was a foreign imperialist power and gave painful caesarean birth to the Chinese Catholic Patriotic Association: henceforth bishops would be appointed by the chairman rather than by the pope. I wanted to ask how long it would take changing China to rebuild the road to Rome. If all of China feels a bit of a time warp like looking at those faded photogravures of your grandparents—then the Catholic Church appears to have spent the last 30 years "on hold" waiting for the rest of the family to come back on the line.

Nancy's Story

Nancy is 24 years old, works as a travel guide at the average Chinese monthly salary of $40, speaks charming lisplike English and lives with her parents and two brothers in a $10-a-month flat. She has a wish list that includes a refrigerator, washing machine, TV and motor bike. She worships nature but not God.

Nancy and her boyfriend are waiting until they are 25 to marry and have the one child allowed by the government; those who wait get maternity leave with pay for 6 months instead of 30 days. Of course, they are as worried as the rest of the child-loving Chinese (less than 14 percent of whom are communist and even fewer of whom are Catholics) that China's one-child quota may create a generation of spoiled brats and problems worse than hunger.

Nancy speaks proudly of the 1949 founding of the People's Republic of China by Mao Tse Tung. She says "Mao accomplished much good for our people but became a little senile in later years." She describes the so-called "cultural revolution" of 1966–76 as "crazy time," anti-cultural paranoia when Mao eliminated all intellectual and spiritual leaders as imagined threats. Nancy claims the Chinese people are just now recovering their human values, rediscovering real love and marriage as more than a working partnership. Nancy is hopeful but not yet happy.

PARABLE OF THE CHINA CHICKS

Just when I was ready to leave China with all the answers, God sent me a parable about wisdom:

An old man—ancient China incarnate—was hobbling across the gravel train yard trying to catch a train about to leave. He was limping and out of breath and carrying a big, awkward box with both hands. Suddenly he stumbled; the box went flying, and out onto the tracks spilled 20 tiny yellow chicks scurrying off in every direction. A caring Christian and take-action American wanted to rush over and help him gather up the lost chicks.

The old man was wiser. He calmly reached into his pocket, pulled out a handful of chicken feed, sprinkled it on the ground, waited a moment for the chicks to hurry back for the feed and then bent over, scooped them all up in his box and boarded the train for home.

THAILAND

A T A GLANCE   THAILAND

Population: *Thailand 55,000,000*
Capital With Population: *Bangkok 5,470,000*
Language: *Thai*
Literacy: *84%*
Faith Expression: *Buddhist 53%, Moslem 47%*
Roman Catholic 5%, in country the size of Texas.
Currency Used: *Baht*
Cities I Visited: *Bangkok*

POSTCARD REFLECTIONS

If elephant power was replaced by human power in Thailand, now human power has been replaced by horsepower. Or the infamous Thai "Tuk-Tuks" (named for the putt-putt sound they make): a 3 wheeler motorcycle taxi chariot rumbleseat—which costs next to nothing (except your life).

"Elephants," says I, "Give me elephants!"

And they grew 'em on trees!

"Excuse me, miss, can you direct me to the fresh vegetable section..."

"Sorry folks, can I get my basket through here, please...?"

MR. CHAINARONG MON-THIENVICHIENCHAI: tall, dark, handsome, brilliant, articulate, generous, President of St. John's College (17,000 students), news anchorman for Thailand's Channel 5 network news and President of UNDA World (UNDA = Latin word for waves— refers to the airwaves which carry religious broadcasts). This media professional is the active Walter Cronkite of Thailand and the Catholic layman you wish you could clone.

MRS. SIRIWAN SAN-TISAKULTARM: industrious, imaginative, deeply committed to her vocation as wife and mother of two and to her profession as producer-writer-investigative reporter for a daily prime time 3-5 minute feature on children's and family issues for Channel 9 network TV...also active in religious communication internationally...a pert and intense telejournalist who is also a courageous Catholic witness.

FR. JEAN HABERSTROH: "old pro" priest communications director who knows how to encourage, inspire, and make others look good.

The Thai people brag about their governor, a vegetarian, who takes no salary, works 12 hours a day and eats only one meal a day (at noon). I have since learned that all Thai people eat only one meal a day: it starts with fried rice & pork soup at 5 a.m.—& never stops til 12 midnight.

99

THAILAND

CREATIVE
COMMUNICATING

IDEAS IN MEDIA MINISTRY

PROFILES
Creative Communicators

FR. ANTHONY:
young, dynamic priest-editor-in-chief of Bangkok's "Catholic news publication" which is a colorful magazine. In most parts of the world the most effective, best read Catholic publications are magazines (not newspapers) which enjoy "shelf-life" (people keep them around the house) and have the ability to give background context to today's breaking religious news stories.

SR. PRAPIN VIRASLIP:
the fun, friendly, creative, caring, committed coordinator and religious woman every media department in the Catholic world wishes it had...working with a superb team of videographers, audio producers, graphic artists, musicians, and support staff who make media miracles happen: from a training institute to a network TV special.

Consultation conference with Fr. Anthony and Bangkok's Catholic Publication Department heads. . . (weekly paper: 2,000, monthly magazine: 5,000)

In my communications workshops I always emphasize the 6 P's — personal, particular, pictoral, parable, positive, and pastoral — in other words what we need are not "animals" but "elephants". Lately I'm realizing the importance of having a person or two on the elephant!

PARABLE OF THE THAI TUK-TUK

Everyone was surprised by the Master's updated metaphor: "Life is like a motor car."

They waited in silence, knowing that an explanation would not be long in coming.

"Oh yes," he said at length. "A motor car can be used to travel to the heights."

Another silence.

"But most people lie in front of it, allow it to run over them, then blame it for the accident."

BANGLADESH

A T A GLANCE   BANGLADESH

Population: *Bangladesh 110,000,000*
Capital With Population: *Dhaka 4,480,000*
Language: *Bengali, English*
Literacy: *25%*
Faith Expression: *Islam 80%, Hindu 16%*
Currency Used: *Taka*
Cities I Visited: *Dhaka*

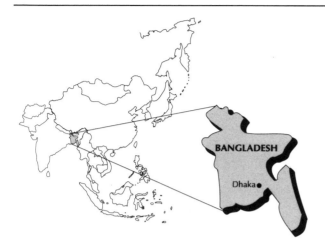

It was sticky, icky hot — couldn't stop dripping since Bangladesh Air landed late at night — worked with my media workshop hosts & crew next day: great spirit and energy...but equipment hard to get (all electric power in downtown Dhaka went off for 30 minutes—& does often!)...1 day for bishops, 3 days for leaders.

POSTCARD
REFLECTIONS

In Bangladesh the floods and accompanying evils (like snakes, drownings, hunger & homelessness) are killing the people.

Just a month before my arrival, floods flashed through 2/3rds of the homes in Bangladesh—leaving 30 million homeless . . . & carrying rats & poisonous snakes to within inches of people's raised beds-on-bricks!

People homeless due to floods, poverty and density of population (worst in world) . . . food is scarce (lots of rice), basics are sparse, people are proud and keep bouncing back! They are teaching me about life — and human values — and priorities & love.

In India the people—Moslems vs Hindus, rebels vs government — are killing each other. Government-controlled TV news is a laundry list of riots, curfews and rebellions.

In a hotel bathroom:

Is forbitten to steal hotel towels please. If you are not person to do such thing is please not to read notis.

Traffic in downtown Dhaka must be the most terrifying in the world.

FR. JYOTI GOMEZ: director, founding father and spiritual godfather of the Christian Communications Center, kind, clever, knows the culture, knows how to build a team and run a big company: from printing, publishing and print sales to radio and TV production and training—all in amazingly adequate studios and office facilities right in the heart of bustling mad Dhaka: his secret is a dedicated staff—like Sisters Shanta and Edward, and engineer Topon—who are as comfortable praying together as they are producing together.

ARCHBISHOP MICHAEL ROSARIO: strong, wise leader and gentle gentleman who supports communications at every level and creates a spirit of caring teamwork that infects the whole church in Dhaka.

FR. JOE BEIXOTTO, C.S.C: busy, bright, President of Notre Dame College in Dhaka—the Fr. Ted Hesberg of Bangladesh, whose wall poster of Knute Rockne and supply of orange drink and peanut butter made me feel at home—although Fr. Joe and many of his faculty and students were out in Bangladesh's annual flood waters on long boats delivering food and comfort to some of the 30 million left homeless.

103

BANGLADESH

CREATIVE
COMMUNICATING

IDEAS IN MEDIA MINISTRY

COMMUNICATIONS IN BANGLADESH

Catholic Communications—or the Catholic Church which is communications—faces an annual crisis or opportunity with the infamous killer floods that thaw down from the Himalayan Mountains near India and China and rage across this poorest densest country in the world on their torrential way to the Bay of Bengal and the Indian Ocean. The floods wipe out crops, animals, people and their mud-brick hovels and there is no escape. People sleep on rooftops and hilltops and pray that their children won't be swept away or bitten by the poisonous snakes also caught in the rushing waters and searching for refuge. Floods also knock down walls, and Muslims, Hindus and Christians huddle together for survival and fight together against heat, bugs, hunger, homelessness, poverty, powerlessness, government corruption and tougher enemies like despair. The world's poorest may also be the world's bravest. There are many media available to the Church: comic books and puppets for a pre-literate people—and, perhaps most creatively, "bell towers" which begin each day at 4:45 am.

Like the Moslem mosques with their electronic amplified loudspeakers on top of every mosque calling (loudly) all people within earshot to prayer five times a day — some Catholic Churches of Bangladesh (about a half dozen so far) have installed their own church bell tower "broadcasting station" which offers a sunrise music & meditation morning prayer. . . well received by Christians and Moslems alike. Also a good form of evangelization outreach which also makes the few Catholics pleased and proud!

Many of the Catholic Bishops of Bangladesh are Holy Cross priests or Notre Dame graduates . . . As another alumnus of Knute Rochne's alma mater I felt among brothers and sisters . . .

104

Participants in a practical hands-on three-day radio workshop in Dhaka.

PARABLE OF FEEDING

There was a dedicated old priest who always wondered what the real difference was between heaven and hell. To satisfy his curiosity, he used to pray for some sort of revelation. One day God granted him the privilege.

He first visited hell. He was absolutely flabbergasted to find no flames, no pointed-tail devils. Only groups of angry people crowding around long wooden picnic tables. Each place had a large wooden bowl of food and a ten foot long wooden spoon.

By pushing themselves into a place at the table and standing on the bench, people managed to get their pool-cleaner-like spoons into the bowls; but they were unable to turn the spoon around and get it into their mouths. That frustration and accompanying bitterness and bickering were apparently the hell of it.

The old priest was then allowed a glimpse of heaven. He was amazed to discover the same massive wooden picnic tables, huge wooden bowls, and ten foot long wooden spoons. But in heaven there was a spirit of peace, thoughtfulness—even joy.

In heaven, the people were feeding each other.

INDIA: Calcutta

AT A GLANCE   *INDIA*
Calcutta Population: *9,900,000*
Currency Used: *Rupee*
Language: *Hindi, English, Bengali,*
Gujarati, Kashmiri, Malayalam,
Marathi, Oriya, Punjabi, Tamil,
Telugu, Urdu, Kannada, Assames
Literacy: *36%*
Faith: *Hindu 83%; Islam 11%;*
Christian 3%; Sikh 2%

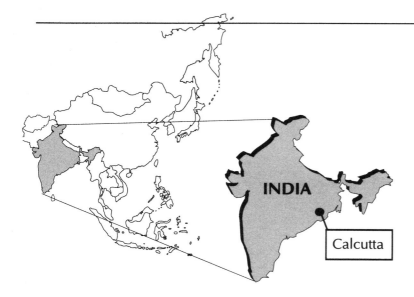

INDIA

Calcutta

India: land of the spiritual — shrines, temples, mosques, churches, candles, incense, garlands, sacred song & dance: ancient culture, family tradition, faith in God, the arts, charity, hospitality ("The guest is God!").

2.00   भारत INDIA   भारत INDIA

POSTCARD
R E F L E C T I O N S

Marriages arranged by the parents are still the common practice in India (most work 'cuz mom knows best & males are revered as near deities): huge dowries are then demanded of the bride's family. She is later beaten & killed if the family does not deliver. Local religious told of three such examples at one of my workshops. A cow or your life.

Just as there are naked children living on the streets of this "City of Joy," people bathing at corner hydrant-like water pumps, scrounging for garbage scraps . . . so, too, there are rats as big as shoe boxes and hungry!

The saddest story from Calcutta is that some of the beggars' babies are deliberately maimed and mutilated so they will become more persuasive beggars!

Smiles to go

Scene: St. Peter's pearly gates.
Archbishop is assigned to modest shack. Skinny, intense young Indian man is rushed into huge heavenly mansion. St. Pete explains: "Archbishop, that man was a Calcutta cab driver — he made more people turn to God in one day than you did in your whole life."

ARCHBISHOP HENRY D'SOUZA:
urbane, witty, charming Archbishop of Calcutta with a deep sense of humanity and humor and hope, who also serves the Catholic Bishops' Conference of India as episcopal moderator of communications—himself a master communicator!

SR. MIRABELLE, A. C:
lovely, loving, superior general of the Apostolic Carmel Sisters...one of the great, gifted team-players (community conscious) who knows contemporary communications (how to listen) and reaches out to others (is not afraid to hug) and continues communication (doesn't forget when you leave). The Apostolic Carmel Sisters help the poor, especially young women, through skits and plays on social issues, occasional TV shows or published articles on dowry-deaths and Sati practices, and even teach literacy for rickshaw pullers and modern math made fun to tribal children.

When you visit a house for the first time in India they often greet you with a garland of flowers (like Hawaiian lei), a red rouge mark on your forehead & 3 sacred bowls: of incense, flower petals and a lit candle. They bless you with each. They also do this during the offertory at Mass.

INDIA: Calcutta

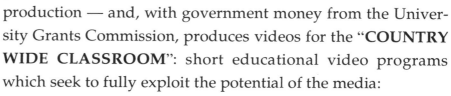

CREATIVE
COMMUNICATING

FR. GASTON ROBERGE:
true intellectual and zealous manager of "Chitrabani" ("Light and Sound") Communication Center—where, with Fr. George, S. J. and Pranay Dutta and staff of 20, they produce educational films and videos for community schools and agencies, like the "Country Wide Classroom" for educational TV, create programming for Radio Veritas and offer training workshops for church leaders. Fr. Roberge is one of today's theological communicators asking the tough questions about our message, i.e. the content of our religious message. Everyone says "the Good News"—but what does that mean to you? To me? To our Muslim neighbor? Each of us has a deeply personal spiritual faith experience of God...we are like young lovers who both say "I love you" but each means different things! If we cannot agree upon an identity of meaning with one another, how can we communicate with the rest of the world?

IDEAS IN MEDIA MINISTRY

"COUNTRY WIDE CLASSROOM"

Chitrabani, a Jesuit Institute with over 20 on staff, offers training in cinema (8mm production and film criticism), radio, TV production — and, with government money from the University Grants Commission, produces videos for the "**COUNTRY WIDE CLASSROOM**": short educational video programs which seek to fully exploit the potential of the media:

- Immediacy, for bringing to viewers the latest and exciting new findings.

- Omnipresence, for taking the viewers to "where the action is": a research laboratory, a hospital, a village, or a conference.

- Animation and special effects, to help clarify concepts, highlight inherent structures or invisible process, etc.

- Visual power, for a vast variety of things, including demonstrations of all types.

- Intimacy, to involve the viewers and make them a part of the voyage of discovery, of wonder and of enquiry.

Mother Teresa of Calcutta with one of our talented workshop participants and author of the Herald Newspaper article: **"You're On Camera One, Dear Bishop."**

THE HERALD

Heralding Justice, Love and Peace

Vol. CXXIV No. 45   CALCUTTA, FRIDAY, NOVEMBER 18, 1988   60 PAISE

"You're On Camera One, Dear Bishop"

● From ROBIN GOMES, SDB

"Good morning, and welcome to our studio", said Miles.

"Good morning . . . I'm Archbishop Telesphore Toppo."

"What is your opinion about conversion theology?" Miles asked.

"Well, as far as I understand..." began the church leader of Ranchi archdiocese, facing Camera 1 of CB Television studio.

At the other end of the microphone, with his back to the camera, was Miles O'Brien Riley, asking a question which could lead the respondent into a popular controversy.

Bishop Linus Gomes of Baruipur a little later, faced the same camera and was asked, what was the very first change he would make if he were to become Pope today!

Tricky and tempting question that! But it raises eyebrows and stretches the eardrum. Every viewer sits tight to hear what the bishop has to say on that. ... Power of media language and grammar!

Later in the day more interviews with several other bishops and religious Superiors, followed. The interviewer was Miles O'Brien Riley, a Catholic priest from the archdiocese of San Francisco.

The whole enactment was a practice session (but in a realistic mood) of a three-day workshop held at Chitra Bani, Calcutta, from October 25 to 27.

The CBCI commission for Proclamation and Social Communication set up a plan early this year and sent invitations to the bishops and major Religious Superiors all over India. Five zonal centres were assigned for this important seminar:

Calcutta October 25–27 Chitrabani

Madras November 1–3 Santhome

Bangalore November 8–10 Ashirvad

Hyderabad November 15–17 Amruthavani

Bombay November 22–24 Xavier Institute for Communication

Fr. Miles O'Brien Riley has been for over twenty years minister for media. Since the time of his entry into this field, he has proved to be a prolific communicator, author and AV programme producer.

He has written five musical comedies, nine books and hundreds of articles and reviews. He has produced and hosted eight films, and over 1000 television and 3000 radio programmes.

He is on radio and T. V. daily in North California. His articles and shows are syndicated throughout the United States and Canada.

In 1970 Father Miles founded a Communication Centre for the Archdiocese of San Francisco. He has served as Vice President of National Catholic Broadcasters (UNDA+BA) and Syndicators (ACTRS). Governor of the Northern California Academy of the TV Arts and Sciences (NATAS).

Having completed his Ph. D. in Berkeley, he served as associate Pastor in several parishes in North America. Bishop Fulton Sheen had Fr. Miles as his production collaborator for his radio and TV serials on the national network in the late seventies.

Father Miles now tours continents, animating media training programmes, especially for church authorities. During his Sabbatical year 1988-1989 he has undertaken media training programmes for 145 centres in the five continents. Calcutta hosted his 24th media workshop for Bishops and Religious Superiors for North-Eastern India.

Archbishop Henry D'Souza of Calcutta was called next for the TV interview. He faced the camera boldly, answering each question. "He does better as an interviewer..." said a participant.

Bishop J. Rodericks of Jamshedpur enjoyed the interview game; he has inborn spontaneity...good for a media promoter.

Then came Bishop Alphonse D'Souza, Bishop Lucas Sircar, Fr. A. J. Sebastian, Sr. Therese Mary, Sr. Mirabelle, Sr. Lourdes Mary, Sr. Lisa...one after another to face the camera, amidst glowing studio lights.

For several, it was the first appearance before a TV camera. And all proved to be potential AV communicators.

That was Miles O'Brien's method of running this intensive media workshop...practical, involving interview was the key tool. He succeeded in exposing the reality of new communication and the information revolution.

Everyone present felt the impact the media is going to make on present-day society. So, what might be the further implications and what should be the proportionate pastoral media plan for the Church and community in India? A "Make Your Plan" session brought out useful indications towards future communication programming in each respective area:

Your Communication Plan

Your Purpose

Your Assessment

Your Target Audience

Your Main Message

Your Best Medium

Your Action Plan — these were the areas that came under study.

Radio (cassette) ministry is still the cheaper and more personal medium today. A practice session opened new grounds for all. The participating bishops and superiors had to produce a one*minute programme.

At the final stage of the workshop the participants were able to see and listen to some model video clips, radio spots and a film, most of which were produced by Miles O'Brien himself.

Chitra Bani (CB) as the host was a most suitable place for this important seminar. Fr. Gaston Roberge with Fr. George Ponodath, Bro. Carlo and the other team members of the Centre offered the best. This media atmosphere and wholesome facility was essential.

Media is a branch that must be understood well by all: bishops, priests, religious and lay-persons. Fr. Miles O'Brien Riley brought home the message: "If St. Paul were alive today, he wouldn't just be writing letters..."

PARABLE OF ANOTHER MOTHER TERESA

It intrigued the congregation to see their rabbi disappear each week on the eve of the sabbath. They suspected he was secretly meeting the Almighty, so they deputed one of their number to follow him. This is what the man saw: the rabbi disguised himself in peasant clothes and served a paralyzed Gentile woman in her cottage, cleaning out the room and preparing a sabbath meal for her.

When the spy got back the congregation asked, "Where did the rabbi go? Did he ascend to heaven?"

"No," the man replied, "he went even higher."

INDIA: Madras

A T A GLANCE   INDIA

Madras Population: 4,900,000
Currency Used: *Rupee*
Language: *Hindi, English, Bengali, Gujarati, Kashmiri, Malayalam, Marathi, Oriya, Punjabi, Tamil, Telugu, Urdu, Kannada, Assames*
Literacy: *36%*
Faith: *Hindu 83%; Islam 11%; Christian 3%; Sikh 2%*

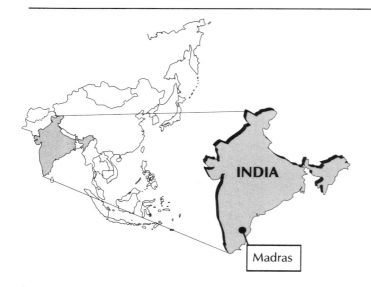

Madras

Madras is more like a Polynesian Island than Southeast India. Balmy breezes (still lotsa sweaty humidity), palm trees and ocean but 1 K. away. While I was there I visited **Mohandas** (more popularly called Mahatma) **Gandhi Shrine Memorial.** Decent and moving: a man of his times and culture.

The state of Tamil Nadu (one of India's 28+ independent states—really each one is a country in area and population!) often enjoys monsoons . . .

POSTCARD
REFLECTIONS

And now the bad news: I had to share this lovely sea-front beach a mile from the media center with the live and dead bodies of dogs, cows, water buffalo and thousands of "squatters" doing their morning ablutions: Toilet and Tomb.

110

From an information booklet about using a hotel air conditioner:

Cooles and Heates:

If you want just condition of warm in your room, please control yourself.

The Bleeding Cross of St. Thomas

FR. VICTOR SUNDERAJ: super-pro, clever, kind, gifted linguist, pioneer-developer of Santhome Communications Center production and training center in central Madras, serving 12 dioceses in the state of Tamil Nadu. Producing radio programs, sound slide shows, photography and edu-communication. In addition to teaching media workshops all over Asia and serving as leader of international communication groups such as UNDA & OCIC, Fr. Victor had the vision to buy a large property and rent out much of it to generate media ministry subsidy support—and the even greater vision to make traditional Indian dance (training and performing) an integral part of the Church's overall communication/evangelization outreach.

St. Thomas, the doubting apostle of Jesus, spent his last years in Madras (just try to doubt it!). His relics are everywhere (enough bones for a family!). There is a Portuguese influence: art, colors, architecture — and Thomas' doubting faith!

INDIA: Madras

FR. ANTHONY KIRUPAKARAN: gentle, compassionate, talented, well educated (several years of graduate communications training in the U.S.), example of the new breed of religious communicator emerging worldwide, now moving up to take Fr. Victor's place as director of Santhome to bring new skills and vision.

MRS. JENNIFER ARUL: gracious, lovely, sharp professional communicator who volunteers to help with Church communications. Almost all our workshops worldwide involved on-camera, on-microphone exercises to teach the church leaders practical experience articulating the Good News—and we always tried to get a woman reporter to conduct our televised "ambush interviews," especially with the bishops. Jennifer was one of the best!

Superb workshop in Madras, India. 3 days with 15 bishops and religious superiors — 2 days with 14 diocesan directors of communications.

IDEAS IN MEDIA MINISTRY

CREATIVE
COMMUNICATING

Catholic communicators in India use folk media—from puppetry and mime, fables and folksongs to traditional dance and theatre—to tell of God's love. They use posters, flannelgraphs, booklets, slide-tape shows, video and audio cassettes, dance troupes and schools, mobile film units and some on-air broadcast.

Helping the bishops of Tamil Nadu improve their communication skills.

At the workshop . . .

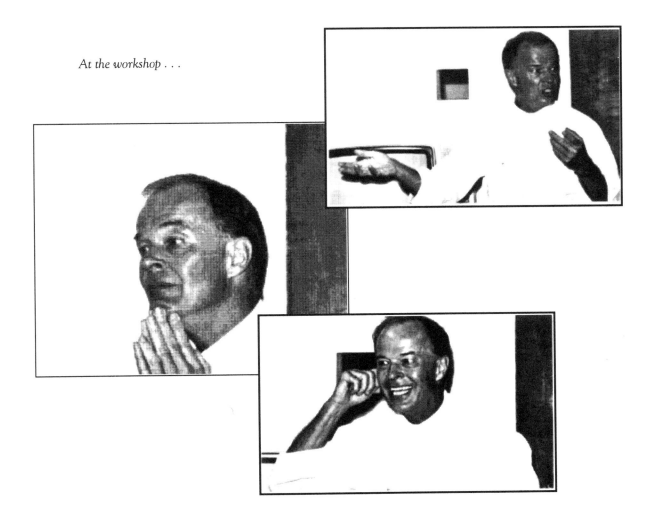

PARABLE OF LISTENING

Here is a prayer of listening I discovered in Madras: "Hark, listen to the song of the bird, the wind in the trees, the ocean roar; look at a tree, a falling leaf, a flower, as if for the first time. You might suddenly make contact with that Paradise from which we, having fallen in childhood, are excluded by our knowledge."

INDIA: Bangalore

A T A GLANCE   **INDIA**

Bangalore Population: *3,900,000*
Currency Used: *Rupee*
Language: *Hindi, English, Bengali,*
Gujarati, Kashmiri, Malayalam,
Marathi, Oriya, Punjabi, Tamil,
Telugu, Urdu, Kannada, Assames
Literacy: *36%*
Faith: *Hindu 83%; Islam 11%;*
Christian 3%; Sikh 2%

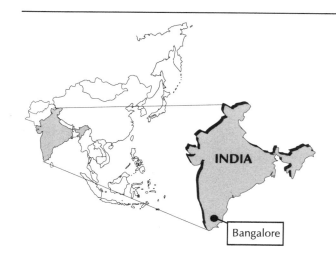

There is a huge inscription chiseled on the facade of this beautiful state capitol: "Government work is God's work"—I ran by it every morn on my meditation/jog—and wondered. Of course, the Indians also say that "the husband is God"... so ... the pressure is on!

Statue of Lord Gomateshwara, over 52 feet tall!

POSTCARD
REFLECTIONS

SMILES to go

In a hotel:

Because of the impropriety of entertaining guests of the opposite sex in the bedroom, it is suggested that the lobby be used for this purpose.

I stayed with Fr. Tony Coelho, S.J., the psychologist - author - counsellor - retreat - master. He took me on a rickshaw tour of the city. Tony's ashram here is named: "Ashirvad" ("Blessing").

Hindu seven-tiered levels of life...(from the bottom up:) earth, water, fire, air, ether, consciousness and God.

PROFILES
Creative Communicators

FR. JOE NAIDU, S.J:
the gentle giant — tallest, most thoughtful Jesuit in India, has integrated the Media Center into the College Campus and curriculum-production facilities, audio recording studios, are teaming with energetic young life.

ARCHBISHOP MATTHIAS:
natural leader, warm friend, episcopal coordinator of Catholic Communications in India and sensitive communicator himself.

FR. TONY COELHO, S.J:
is blessed with the unique gift of humility, able to be authentically himself—learned, insightful, witty author - lecturer - spiritual director—and, at the same time, modest and unpretentious: another radical reminder that what we ultimately communicate is ourselves. His staff at the Ashirvad ("Blessing") Center—Brothers Paul and Filippo, Mary, Hilda, Prestina, Flavia—provided not only lecture halls and video studios for our workshops—but a home: full of light, love, dance, celebration.

INDIA: Bangalore

LIKE WATER OFF A LOTUS BLOSSOM

I never handled being a rich kid very well. I was embarrassed by my family's mansion, what with the gardeners, butlers and maids. I made the chauffeur drop me off a block from school or baseball practice so the other kids wouldn't tease me. I wore the same jacket for the first five years in the seminary and never invited anyone home. I was in my 20's before I realized what my parents knew perfectly well: what matters isn't how much you have, but what you do with it.

In Jerusalem they tell of the gate now walled in called "The Eye of the Needle," a low, narrow gate leading to the Holy City. For a camel to pass through the Eye of the Needle, it had to kneel down and take off the saddle bags, which is precisely what a rich man needs to do to enter the kingdom of Heaven: worship God and strip off the baggage.

When I was packing my bags for this communications pilgrimage around the world, I decided to practice a little detachment. My plan was to give away all the "things" cluttering up my life and drive away from St. Gabriel's with only what I could throw into my car. The night before I left, I sold the car to a dear parishioner. A few "things" were stored in a guest room closet at St. Gabriel's, but mostly I became free, unencumbered by baggage. Or detached, as they say here in India, like water off a lotus blossom.

What a liberating — if terrifying — experience it was to travel with a few books, videos and clothes (which became fewer as stuff wore out and climates got hotter). Totally dependent on the gracious hospitality of our 2000 year old, 850 million-member Catholic family. Asia teaches the need to travel light, to sort out values, to discover the real treasures of the earth. Japan paying dearly for its industrial wealth. China sacrificing family for economic values. Bangladesh, resilient but repeatedly flooded: homes, crops, animals, little babies swept away in the deluge. India torn in half: 400 million hurting, hungry — 400 million healthy, happy. These struggling nations provoke questions: What is life all about? What is worth struggling for? Dying for? Living for?

Asia's answer is spiritual: ancient culture, the arts, family traditions, faith in God, charity, hospitality (in India they say, "The guest is God"), shrines, temples, mosques, churches, candles, incense, garlands, sacred song and dance, a keen awareness of the religious roots of human existence. And India, with its dhyan, or centered meditation (it later becomes Indian yoga and Chinese zen), may be the most spiritually wealthy nation in Asia.

CREATIVE
COMMUNICATING

MEDIA CENTER

Cleverly and wisely, Fr. Joe Naidu has established his recording studios and media production and training center right in the midst of a large school and a Jesuit faculty house, bringing together experience, expertise and youthful energy—the magic ingredients for successful communication centers worldwide.

PARABLE OF GREAT PRICE

Once upon a time, an Indian monk in his travels found a precious stone and kept it. One day he met a traveler, and when he opened his bag to share his provisions with him, the traveler saw the jewel and asked the monk to give it to him. The monk did so readily. The traveler departed, overjoyed with the unexpected gift of the precious stone that was enough to give him wealth and security for the rest of his life. However, a few days later, he came back in search of the monk, found him, gave him back the stone and begged him: "Now give me something much more precious than this stone, valuable as it is. Give me that which enabled you to give it to me."

INDIA: Hyderabad

A T A GLANCE   INDIA

Hyderabad Population: *2,800,000*
Currency Used: *Rupee*
Language: *Hindi, English, Bengali,*
Gujarati, Kashmiri, Malayalam,
Marathi, Oriya, Punjabi, Tamil,
Telugu, Urdu, Kannada, Assames
Literacy: *36%*
Faith: *Hindu 83%; Islam 11%;*
Christian 3%; Sikh 2%

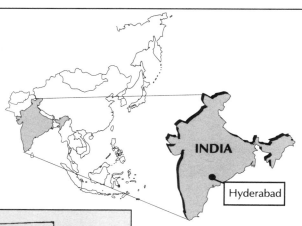

INDIA

Hyderabad

POSTCARD
REFLECTIONS

These mosque towers house huge loud (!) speakers which blare out a call to pray in strident chant every morning at 4:45 a.m. & 4 more times during the day . . . they're not "playing our song."

. . . One of the incredible wonders of India . . . and the world, Golconda fortress, 7 kilometers in circumference which reminds one of China's Great Wall and was the most sturdy in all of India. . . and, in fact, gave birth to the modern city of Hyderabad.

118

SMILES to go

In a hotel lobby:

Visitors are expected to complain at the office between the hours of 9 and 11 A.M. daily.

Amruthavani's magnificent logo of two hands, pierced with Christ's stigmata, symbolize God's eternal wholeness, holiness and blessing—and our human openness and receptivity to receive God's Word.

FR. JULIAN MARINENI: quiet, hospitable, priest director who trusts and delegates, has built a huge operation with over 65 people who pray and work together on radio - video - publishing - and audio - visual supports. Of great interest is their adult religious education (2-year catechetical instruction) through the mail: they attract Hindu and Muslim Indians by radio and then mail easy-to-read catechetical materials to tens of thousands every month for at least two years, until they are ready for baptism.

FR. RAYMOND AMBROSE: gregarious, open, energetic dreamer and one of the most thoughtful hosts in the world: generous with his possessions, his money and, most of all, his time. Good at bringing out the best in others, celebrates daily Mass at an orphanage of 200 homeless kids who call him "father" and love him like "daddy."

INDIA: Hyderabad

FIVE PARABLES ON PRAYER

The Indian guru sat with his disciples in the audience. He said, "You have heard many a prayer and said many a prayer. Tonight I should like you to see one." At that moment the curtain rose, and the ballet began.

* * *

A dervish was asked why he worshipped God through dance. "Because," he replied, "to worship God means to die to self; dancing kills the self. When the self dies, all problems die with it. Where the self is not, love is, God is."

* * *

The rule in one Indian monastery was not "Do not speak" but "Do not speak unless you can improve on the silence." Might not the same be said of prayer? Gandhi put it this way: "It is better in prayer to have a heart without words than words without a heart."

* * *

An old Indian man would sit motionless for hours on end in church. One day a priest asked him what he talked to God about. "I don't talk to God. I just listen." "Well then," the priest asked, "what does God say to you?" "God doesn't talk, either. He just listens."

* * *

The four stages of prayer: (1) I talk, you listen; (2) you talk, I listen; (3) neither talks, both listen; (4) neither talks, neither listens: silence.

PARABLE OF SELF-RIGHTEOUS

Indians tell of the pious old man who prayed five times a day while his business partner never set foot in church. On his 80th birthday the old man prayed thus: "Oh, God, since I was a youth I have come to church daily, prayed at the required times and constantly invoked your name. Yet here I am, poor as a church mouse. But look at my business partner. He drinks, gambles, consorts with women—and still he's rolling in wealth. I wonder if a single prayer has ever crossed his lips. I do not ask that he be punished, but please, Lord, why have you let him prosper and why do you treat me like this?" "Because," said God in reply, "you are such a monumental bore."

PARABLE OF GOD WILLING

To the disciples' delight the Master said he wanted a new shirt for his birthday. The finest cloth was bought. The village tailor came in to have the Master measured, and promised, by the will of God, to make the shirt within a week.

A week went by and a disciple was dispatched to the tailor while the Master excitedly waited for his shirt. Said the tailor, "There has been a slight delay. But, by the will of God, it will be ready by tomorrow."

Next day the tailor said, "I'm sorry it isn't done. Try again tomorrow and, if God so wills, it will certainly be ready."

The following day the master said, "Ask him how long it will take if he keeps God out of it."

INDIA: Bombay

AT A GLANCE   **INDIA**

Bombay Population: 9,000,000
Currency Used: Rupee
Language: Hindi, English, Bengali,
Gujarati, Kashmiri, Malayalam,
Marathi, Oriya, Punjabi, Tamil,
Telugu, Urdu, Kannada, Assames
Literacy: 36%
Faith: Hindu 83%; Islam 11%;
Christian 3%; Sikh 2%

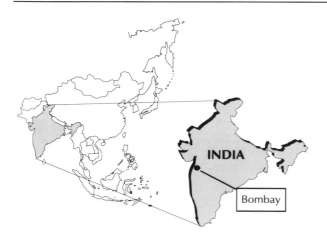

Belles on a Bombay bus!

Bit of a busman's holiday, but spent an afternoon working with 15 college kids on radio (creative scripting and production) at the local studio. . .They made jingles, ads, PSAs and dramas . . . and revealed a great deal of Indian youth (and India) today. Fascinating. Lovely. Classy.

P.S.: Worried about war in Sri Lanka!

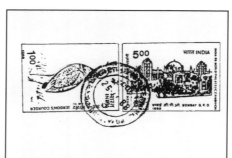

POSTCARD
REFLECTIONS

The key to Christian prayer — and Christian life — was expressed by a bishop in Bombay. He retold the Palm Sunday story of Jesus' donkey ride into Jerusalem amid the happy "hosanna" crowd and over regal palm branches. Apparently the donkey thought that all the fanfare was for him. Contemporary Christ-bearers should know better.

Bombay is the San Francisco of India — in location, climate, openness, cosmopolitan, polyglot, multi-ethnic C.B. deMille cast of characters . . . and one.

122

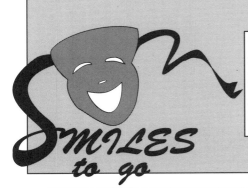

Smiles to go

From the brochure of a car-rental firm:

When passenger of foot heave in sight, tootle the horn. Trumpet him melodiously at first, but if he still obstacles your passage then tootle him with vigor.

FR. GERRY D'ROZARIO, S.J: soft-spoken executive, with a professor's wisdom and a friend's humor; his director's office on the second floor of the Xavier Institute has no desk: only several chairs — all alike — in a circle — a good symbol of how he approaches communication. He merges academic communication instruction with training and A-V production for the local church.

FR. ALBAN DEMELLO, S.J: a tender, caring, fellow Jesuit, professor and teammate communicator—complements Fr. Gerry with his gracious, giving attention to detail—and especially to people!

View from my room at St. Xavier's College.

Xavier Institute enjoys the rich tradition of a beautiful old college in the heart of Bombay's 9,000,000 inhabitants (4,500,000 surviving almost miraculously on the streets) and the youthful energy and enthusiasm of hundreds of students who bring strong hands and hearts, fresh imaginations to the business of religious communicating.

INDIA: Bombay

CREATIVE
COMMUNICATING

XAVIER INSTITUTE OF COMMUNICATIONS

Xavier Institute of Communications is a professional media centre which offers a variety of services in training and production.

The Institute is located in downtown Bombay on the Campus of St. Xavier's College—a premiere educational institution dating back to 1869.

More than 400 students enroll each year in courses like Journalism, Advertising, Public Relations and Visual Media: audiovisuals, video and film production. Specialized workshops attract participants from all over India, from neighbouring countries like Pakistan, Bangladesh and Sri Lanka, and from as far away as Tanzania and The Philippines.

The faculty is drawn from distinguished professionals in the field. Over the years, they have developed an excellent rapport with the student body, which explains the high degree of involvement and participation which characterizes the activities of the Institute.

The alumni are well-placed both in India and abroad. There is scarcely any area of media activity in which they have not made a mark.

By virtue of its course offerings and enrollments, the Xavier Institute of Communications ranks among the biggest non-governmental media centres in Asia.

It was set up in 1969 by the Catholic Bishops' Conference of India to develop scholarship and professionalism in the media.

The Institute is an autonomous educational unit of the Bombay St. Xavier's College Society which comprises St. Xavier's College, the Institute of Management, the Institute of Counselling and the Heras Institute of Indian History and Culture.

The trust is under the management of the Society of Jesus. Inspired by the life and teachings of Christ, the Society has toiled for over 400 years in the field of education because it believes that prevailing social conditions can be transformed.

"We believe that the media are a tremendous power for good or ill, and that whoever is involved with the media should be aware of the relationship between society, individuals and the media.

We attempt to provide an introduction to the media world which emphasizes professionalism and social values relevant to developing nations."

WORKSHOPS

- Video Production: VHS
- Video Production: Umatic
- Video Camera Work: VHS
- Video Camera Work: Umatic
- Video Editing: Umatic
- Audiovisual Production
- Sound Recording Techniques
- Studio Photography Techniques
- Public Speaking
- Announcing, Broadcasting, Compering, Dubbing: English/Hindi

PARABLE OF PRAYER

The governor on his travels stepped in to pay homage to the Master.

"Affairs of state leave me no time for lengthy dissertations," he said. "Could you put essence of religion into a paragraph or two for a busy man like me?"

"I shall put it into a single word for the benefit of your highness."

"Incredible! What is that unusual word?"

"Silence."

"And what is the way to Silence?"

"Meditation."

"And what, may I ask, is meditation?"

"Silence."

INDIA: Goa

A **T A GLANCE**   **INDIA**

Goa Population: *1,500,000*
Currency Used: *Rupee*
Language: *Hindi, English, Bengali,*
Gujarati, Kashmiri, Malayalam,
Marathi, Oriya, Punjabi, Tamil,
Telugu, Urdu, Kannada, Assames
Literacy: *36%*
Faith: *Hindu 83%; Islam 11%;*
Christian 3%; Sikh 2%

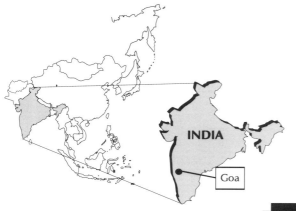

POSTCARD
R E F L E C T I O N S

Old Fort Aguada must be one of the most beautiful beaches in the whole world.

The whole extended family pulls in the catch of the day — for food and the fish market.

126

In a hotel bathroom:

Please to bathe inside the tub.

Smiles to go

VIOLET GOMES: devout believer and top-notch guide in Old Goa who provided one of the great communication moments of the journey. After conducting many tours to the coffin of St. Francis Xavier where his bodily remains lie incorrupt after all these years and after trying to answer the many impossible (and even ridiculous) questions of visiting pilgrims, Violet called us all to attention before leaving the bus and explained crisply: "St. Francis' body is still here! This is what is called a miracle! A miracle means that there is no explanation!"

The Basilica of Bom Jesus 1605 where St. Francis Xavier is entombed.

It bothered me a bit that St. Francis Xavier's statue over the tabernacle on the main altar was about 8 times larger than Jesus' statue — until I realized that Jesus got top billing on the church: "Bom Jesus".

The silver casket of the miraculously preserved relics of St. Francis Xavier.

PARABLE OF THE MIRACLE

A man traversed land and sea to check for himself the Master's extraordinary fame.

"What miracles has your Master worked?" he said to a disciple.

"Well, there are miracles and there are miracles. In your land it is regarded as a miracle if God does someone's will. In our country it is regarded as a miracle if someone does the will of God."

INDIA: Cochin

AT A GLANCE   **INDIA**

Cochin Population: *1,200,000*
Currency Used: *Rupee*
Language: *Hindi, English, Bengali, Gujarati, Kashmiri, Malayalam, Marathi, Oriya, Punjabi, Tamil, Telugu, Urdu, Kannada, Assames*
Literacy: *36%*
Faith: *Hindu 83%; Islam 11%; Christian 3%; Sikh 2%*

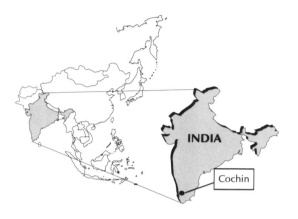

A colorful performer from the Kathakali Dance in Kerala.

POSTCARD
REFLECTIONS

The Taj Mahal in Agra is a glistening white "labor for love."

FR. GEORGE AND FR. THOMAS: scholars and superb communicators who also have big hearts and open hospitality, and in the world-famous Kerala spirit of kindness, make their Pastoral Orientation Center a place of learning and love.

CREATIVE COMMUNICATING

IDEAS IN MEDIA MINISTRY

Pastoral Orientation Center

The church in India provides many superb Christian formation centers — which offer courses in religious education, contemporary spirituality, pastoral ministry and modern mass media. No area of India is more Catholic than the State of Kerala. Cochin is the capital, and the Pastoral Orientation Center is the training nerve center.

This is the chapel of the Ashram/Retreat/Training Center where we held our Cochin Kerala (Southern India) workshops.

PARABLE OF DESTRUCTION

Much advance publicity was made for the address the Master would deliver on "The Destruction of the World" and a large crowd gathered at the monastery grounds to hear him.

The address was over in less than a minute. All he said was: "These things will destroy the human race: politics without principle, progess without compassion, wealth without work, learning without silence, religion without fearlessness and worship without awareness."

SINGAPORE

AT A GLANCE   **SINGAPORE**

Population: 2,668,000
Capital With Population: Singapore 2,350,000
Language: Chinese, Malay, Tamil, English
Literacy: 84%
Faith Expression: Buddhist, Taoist, Moslem, Hindu, Christian
Currency Used: Singapore-dollar
Cities I Visited: Singapore

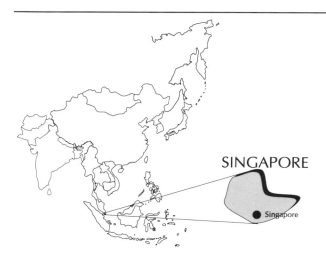

Took a kind of smoke break in Singapore after successful workshops in Malaysia . . . in transit to Jakarta, capital of Indonesia.

130

Smiles to go

In the office of a doctor:

Specialist in women and other diseases.

In a shop:

Our nylons cost more than common, but you'll find they are best in the long run.

The Communication Center in Singapore gave me two albums of photos they had taken of me teaching workshops and seminars. Never have I seen me so happy, centered, at peace. I looked at the two books of pictures and realized: there is a man doing what God wants him to do.

131

SINGAPORE

CREATIVE
COMMUNICATING

Singapore Catholic Audiovisual Center

The Singapore Catholic Audiovisual Center is never quiet: young people are working on a new video or radio program or slide-tape show or Catholic families (many paying members of the AV Family) are stopping by to rent a video or audio cassette from the Media Resource Library. The center offers 16mm films, filmstrips, slide library, audio talks, music tapes, records, audio and video dubbing services, video library and distribution, sound slide productions, video editing, compact disc, training courses and workshops.

New Ad Ed TV Channel

Singapore will launch in 1998 a channel exclusively for adult education to teach languages and career skills. (AMIC, Vol. 9/3)

Singapore knows how to organize workshops: for priests and sisters in the morning, for teachers and young people in the afternoon, and for parents and families in the evening — with creative productions tucked in between

PARABLE OF THE OPEN BOOK

The Master claimed he had a book that contained everything one could conceivably know about God.

No one had ever seen the book till a visiting scholar, by dint of persistent entreaty, wrested it from the Master. He took it home and eagerly opened it—only to find that every one of its pages was blank.

"But the book says nothing," wailed the scholar.

"I know," said the Master contentedly. "But see how much it indicates!"

MALAYSIA

A T A GLANCE   MALAYSIA

Population: 15,070,000 ('87)
Capital with population: Kuala Lumpur
          450,000
Literacy: 75%
Faith: Moslem 50%; Buddhist 26%; Hindu 9%
Currency: Ringgit
Language: Bahasa Malaysia, Chinese

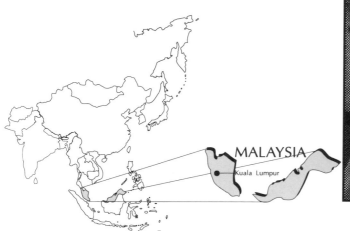

Some Malaysian Bishops practice on-camera press briefings while others role-play the press corps.

Black boards and white boards are often as pedagogically useful as microphones and cameras.

CREATIVE
COMMUNICATING

ASEAN NETWORK

The ASEAN nations (Malaysia, Brunei, Indonesia, Singapore, Thailand and the Philippines) are building a U.S. $250 million ASEAN Optical Fibre Submarine Cable Network. By 1991 the first three segments will connect Brunei, Malaysia, Singapore and the Philippines. By 1995, when the entire network will be completed, it will link all ASEAN countries.

MAJOWE CENTER

The Majowe Center, dream and creation of Bishop James Chan in 1980, includes: a chapel, two A-V studios with excellent equipment, a library, an auditorium, a printing shop with computerized typesetting and a darkroom, which has published catechisms, hymnals, prayer books and bulletins.

PROFILES
Creative Communicators

BISHOP JAMES CHAN OF JOHOR:
lively, hospitable, passionately committed to the media ministry—gives generously of his resources and support.

MR. SAMSON IRUDAYAM:
Director of the Catholic Communications Center in Kuala Lumpur and one of the great personal communicators in Asia. He puts people first, is a great host, letter writer, workshop leader, and imaginative, questioning evangelizer.

PARABLE OF THE BLESSING

A grocer came to the Master in great distress to say that across the way from his shop they had opened a large chain store that would drive him out of business. His family had owned his shop for a century—and to lose it now would be his undoing, for there was nothing else he was skilled at.

Said the Master, "If you fear the owner of the chain store, you will hate him. And hatred will be your undoing."

"What shall I do?" said the distraught grocer.

"Each morning walk out of your shop onto the sidewalk and bless your shop, wishing it prosperity. Then turn to face the chain store and bless it too."

"What? Bless my competitor and destroyer?"

"Any blessing you give him will rebound to your good. Any evil you wish him will destroy you."

After six months the grocer returned to report that: 1) he had had to close down his shop as he had feared, 2) he was now in charge of the chain store, 3) his affairs were in better shape than ever before.

INDONESIA: Jakarta

A T A GLANCE   *Indonesia*

Population: *160,000,000*
Language: *Indonesian; Javanese; English; Dutch, and more than 60 regional languages.*
Literacy: *64%*
Faith Expression: *Muslem 90%, Christian 5%*
Currency Used: *Rupiah*
Capital with Population: *Jakarta: 8,000,000*

350 years of Dutch Colonial Control (1650–1945) with a few years of British control (during 1830's when Raffles and others introduced English essentials like left hand drive and tea) have left their mark on the land of contrasts now 90%+ Muslem with only remnants of Dutch churches and language.

POSTCARD
REFLECTIONS

150,000,000 Indonesians live on the island of Java (in big cities like Jakarta, Yogyakarta, and Surabaya) — only 75–80,000,000 others live on the other 12,999 islands: like Bali, Sumatra or Flores (which is all Catholic). The Javanese speak their own language (Javanese) and "Indonesian" (a kind of Esperanto for all the Indonesian languages) and then English.

SMILES to go

In a hotel elevator:

> Do not enter the lift backwards, and only when lit up.

The temple reflects the four levels of all human life:
1. *Life in the world*
2. *Life in Buddha—prayer, love, sacrifice*
3. *Spiritual life (without bodies and forms)*
4. *Nirvana—Ecstasy, detachment, heaven, God*

An elaborately etched orangutan skull by Kenyah people in Indonesia Borneo.

Please don't miss the Catholic cathedral (we're 3% of the 180,000 population, mostly Muslim, in Indonesia) tucked in behind the main Mosque in the capital, Jakarta! Ah, religious freedom!!

PROFILES
Creative Communicators

FR. BOSCO BEDING, S.V.D: truly a sweet and gentle man, a caring conscientious communicator, and maybe a modern martyr. As director of the National Bishops' Communication Committee, Fr. Bosco was appointed to a national film board. That a Catholic priest could hold such high office apparently angered some — and Fr. Bosco's lifeless body was found along the road. He was a most solicitous host — even pushing me to a dentist when my tooth broke — and became a dear friend. I know that God had special hospitality waiting in heaven — and special music which was Bosco's contribution to mass evangelization.

137

INDONESIA: Jakarta

FR. A.S. BRONTODARSONO, S.J:
quick, articulate, with a twinkle in the eye, "Broto" is one of the "Old Pro's" of Catholic Communication in Indonesia and founding father of a large active mass media enterprise called Sanggar Prathivi Foundation: with slide-tape, video studios and production, several air quality audio recording studios (used round-the-clock by Javanese traditional music groups) a publishing house, printing press, bookstore, and many publications.

MRS. ITA INDRASANA:
charming, intelligent executive producer at Sanggar Prathivi who also belongs to a charismatic renewal group—she and her husband are examples of Lumen 2000 at its best—so that faith spills over into communication.

CREATIVE
COMMUNICATING

IDEAS IN MEDIA MINISTRY

Catholic Communication Overview In Indonesia

31 of the 33 Catholic dioceses of Indonesia have communication centers and media ministry directors—27 were present at our National UNDA Conference and Study Days at Prigen, near Surabaya. 7 have publishing houses, 8 have printing presses, 8 have bookstores, 27 have national or diocesan magazines, 8 have special bulletins, 12 have audio recording studios, 6 have video and/or film studios, 13 have their own radio stations.

Inspiring in both quantity and quality of their productions, several were played publicly at our conference for group evaluation.

PANCASILA

PANCA=Five SILA=Principle; 5 basic principles of
Indonesian State ideology:
1. Belief in God
2. Humanism
3. Nationalism
4. Democracy
5. Social Justice;
Ideology as in "Ideal"

In India, you pull up at a red light and the beggars besiege your car, pound on the windows and put their worst, most pitiable foot (or stump) forward. In Indonesia, the kids approach your car, whip out a rag and pretend to clean the windows or the hood—then they ask for the handout!

What I love most about Indonesian architecture is the earthy, natural way it brings the out-of-doors indoors: in gardens, ponds, waterfalls, & rock formations in the atriums or front halls — with streams, little lawns, trees, & shrubs in the living, dining, and sleeping areas. Everything is open: nature crosses the threshold. Creation and creativity intersect. As few walls as possible!

PARABLE OF THE DEAD BUDDHA

On a cold winter night a wandering ascetic asked for shelter in a temple. The poor man stood shivering there in the falling snow so the temple priest, reluctant though he was to let the man in, said, "Very well, you can stay but only for the night. This is a temple, not a hospice. In the morning you will have to go."

At dead of night the priest heard a strange crackling sound. He rushed to the temple and saw an incredible sight. There was the stranger warming himself at a fire he had lit in the temple. A wooden Buddha was missing. The priest asked, "Where is the statue?"

The wanderer pointed to the fire, then said, "I thought this cold would kill me."
The priest shouted, "Are you out of your mind?" Do you know what you have done? That was a Buddha statue. You have burnt the Buddha!"
The fire was slowly dying out. The ascetic gazed into it and began to poke it with his stick. "What are you doing now?" the priest yelled.
"I am searching for the bones of the Buddha whom you say I burnt."

Some folks still value a dead Buddha over a live man...

INDONESIA: Yogyakarta

A T A GLANCE   *Yogyakarta*
Capital With Population: 7,800,000
Language: *Indonesian*
Literacy: 64%
Faith Expression: 90% Muslim,
    5% Christian
Currency Used: *Rupiah*

My Yogyakarta video team and crew met me at the airport the morning I arrived and rushed me to this incredible Buddhist Temple, so I could touch the Buddha's thumb for good luck (=Blarney Stone?!) & we could pray for the success of our video workshops.

Spent 4 hours one afternoon outside Yogyakarta visiting this immense impressive temple to Buddha (in a land 90% Moslem!), Constructed in the 9th century with every moment and fabled myth in Buddha's life traced in lovely, detailed stone etchings around the outside.

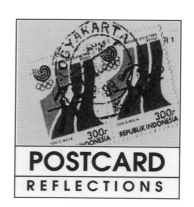

POSTCARD
REFLECTIONS

The entire 9th century temple of Borobudur is a communication tool: teaching the life of Buddha etched in stone panels, which read like cartoon pictures as you circle the temple to the top.

In India and Bangladesh, the bike and the pedaller are in front pulling—here in Indonesia, they are behind pushing—what does that tell you about these cultures?

Detour sign:

Stop: Drive Sideways.

SMILES to go

FR. ALOYSIUS BUDYAPRANTA: smiling, bustling, bringing and being good news, Director of "Komosos Kas" diocesan media center with emphasis on information services and audio cassettes.

FR. RUEDI HOFMAN, S.J.: serious, scholarly, creative, committed— if I were choosing 12 apostles of modern mass media worldwide, Ruedi would be one of the 12 — his Puskat Center enjoys the imaginative skills of over twenty exceptional young communicators including Fred and Yogy.

FR. JOSEPH MANGUNWIJAYA: simple, unaffected, deeply involved with the poor — lived for seven years with homeless in the dirt under a bridge — who uses a popular column in the secular newspapers to tell parables of contemporary justice and injustice.

Fred, Yogy, and Beng-Beng from Puskat Studios take me on a tour of Borobudur, largest Buddhist Temple in Central Java, Indonesia

Indonesia—or, more precisely, the Island of Java where 1/2 the people live,—has fireflies!!! They lit my way tonight as I jogged the Yogyakarta rice paddies after dark—& they reminded me of growing up in Indiana while the Mills Brothers sang: Light Up You Lil' Ole Bug of Lighting: If You Gotta Glow . . .

INDONESIA: Yogyakarta

PUSKAT A-V Studio

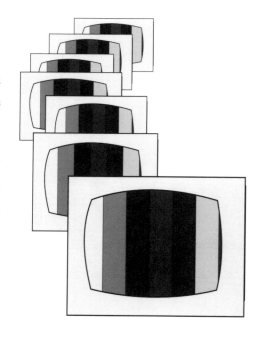

"**Photo Novels**" or "**Photo Novelas**" using a still photo camera, they create an album of photos that tell a story, with words or narrative printed in "Bubbles" as in comic strips.

The Puskat A-V studio is very social justice-oriented in its productions and concentrates on "inexpensive" or group media such as wall magazines, posters, comics, creative drawing, puppets, people's theatre, traditional dance, music, sound slides, audiocassettes—and now lately, video production.

One fascinating production concerns "Borobudur" a famous 9th century Buddhist Temple near Yogyakarta. By explaining the stories carved in stone panels around the temple walls, this 35-minute documentary teaches parables of justice, truth and harmonious human life.

Puskat is a powerful, persuasive voice for the poor.

If there is right in the soul, there will be beauty in the person.
If there is beauty in the person, there will be harmony in the home.
If there is harmony in the home, there will be order in the nation.
If there is order in the nation, there will be peace in the world.

(Lao Tsu 6B.C).

Lawrence of Arabia or Fr. Miles riding
wildly along the shores of Indonesia.

PARABLE OF THE FREED BUDDHA

The Kamakura Buddha was lodged in a temple until one day a mighty storm brought the temple down. Then for many years the massive statue stood exposed to sun and rain and wind and the changes of the weather.

When a priest began to raise funds to rebuild the temple, the statue appeared to him in a dream and said, "That temple was a prison, not a home. Leave me exposed to the ravages of life. That's where I belong."

Jesus didn't spend all his time in the temple either.

INDONESIA: Surabaya

A T A GLANCE   *Surabaya*

Population: *2,400,000*
Language: *Indonesian*
Literacy: *64%*
Faith Expression: *90% Muslim; 5% Christian*
Currency Used: *Rupiah*

Profile of Indonesia.

POSTCARD
REFLECTIONS

We flew at 6 a.m. to Surabaya, Indonesia (after a 2 hr. bus ride from Yogyakarta to the airport): at Surabaya we took another long van ride to Prigen in the mountains of N.E. Java where the Vincentians have a retreat house for 100 which became our workshop venue for 23 days.

Indonesians love theatre and traditional dance. This happy Gambuh dancer and horse perform classical opera .

SMILES to go

In a hotel room:

The flattening of underwear with pleasure is the job of the chambermaid.

Dani tribesmen wear traditional war dress: crowne shells (once the currency of exchange), dog's fur, colorful birds' feathers, and pigs' teeth. Soot and pigs' fat are smeared on the body for health.

EVA PASARIBU: sparkling, smart, dedicated writer-producer working in audio-visual production with KOMSOS—she is a great example of the lay professionals who are developing in church communication in Indonesia. For example, of 33 dioceses in Indonesia, 27 were represented at our Prigen (near Surabaya) National Conference and workshop—and 10 of the 33 have public service access to broadcast TV. Eva writes for four local radio shows: 5 minute morning meditation, 20 minute Sunday sermon, 25 minute "Happy Family" weekly program, and 15 minute weekly children's show.

Eva sums up the fear, frustration and faith feelings of many: *So I have work for 11 years and I love this work very much. I always find many difficult in this job but that is over and I'm happy. So many people (the Catholics) didn't understand this job. And there are many priests too. They always think that this work is "just hobby and just playing the music." Sometimes I'm very sad when the priests (in our archdiocese) did not care about this pastoral. But I know that the mass media is the very important for nowadays.*

Eva Pasaribu is interviewed about her faith and experience of God.

145

INDONESIA: Surabaya

IDEAS IN MEDIA MINISTRY

Communication Training Center

CTC, the large (sleeps 100) Conference Center at Prigen, Surabaya where we met for the National UNDA Indonesia Assembly and Study Days, offers dozens of instructional classes in modern media and pastoral communications. Their excellent 45 page brochure lays a firm common sense foundation of the basic human need for communication:

CREATIVE
COMMUNICATING

WHY WE COMMUNICATE

The need for contact and companionship is just as great for all of us as individuals who have led solitary lives by choice or necessity have discovered. This need for company has been even verified experimentally. In one study of isolation, subjects were paid to remain alone in a locked room. Five of the subjects lasted for eight days. Three held out for two days, one commented, "Never again!" One subject lasted only two hours.

In other words, we all need people. We all need to communicate.

A. PHYSICAL NEEDS

Communication is so important that it is necessary for physical health. In fact, evidence suggests that an absence of satisfying communication can even jeopardize life itself. Medical researchers have identified a wide range of medical hazards that result from a lack of close relationships.
For instance:

- Socially isolated people are two to three times more likely to die prematurely than those with strong social ties.

- Divorced men (before age seventy) die from heart disease, cancer, and strokes at double the rate of married men.

- The rate of all types of cancer is as much as five times higher for divorced men and women, compared to their single counterparts.

- Poor communication can contribute to coronary disease.

- The likelihood of death increases when a close relative dies.

Research like this demonstrates the importance of satisfying personal relationships. Remember: Not everyone needs the same amount of contact, and the quality of communication is almost certainly as important as the quantity. The important point here is that personal communication is essential for our well being.

B. EGO NEEDS

Communication does more than just enable us to survive. It is the way indeed, the only way to learn who we are. Are we smart or stupid, attractive or ugly, skillful or inept? The answers to these questions don't come from looking in the mirror.

We decide how we are based on how others react to us. Deprived of communication with others, we would have no sense of identity, no "self-image."

C. SOCIAL NEEDS

Besides helping define who we are, communication is the way we relate socially with others. A psychologist, William Schutz, describes three types of social needs we strive to fulfill by communicating.

The first is inclusion, the need to feel a sense of belonging to some personal relationship. Inclusion needs are sometimes satisfied by informal alliances: the friends who study together, a group of runners, or neighbors who help one another with yard work. In other cases, we get a sense of belonging from formal relationships: everything from religious congregations to a job to marriage.

A second type of social need is the desire for control — the desire each of us has to influence others, to feel some sense of power over our world. Some types of control are obvious, such as the boss or team captain whose directions make things happen. Much control, however, is more subtle.

The third social need is affection — desire to care for others and know that they care for us. Affection, of course, is critical for most of us. Being included, having power, aren't very satisfying if the important people in our lives don't care for us.

D. PRACTICAL NEEDS

We shouldn't overlook the everyday, important functions communication serves. Communication is the tool that lets us tell the hair stylist to take just a little off the side, the doctor where it hurts, and the plumber that the broken pipe needs attention now!

Communication is the means of learning important information in school.

It is the method you use to convince a prospective employer that you're the best candidate for a job, and it is the way to persuade the boss that you deserve a raise. The list of common but critical jobs performed by communicating goes on and on, and it's worth noticing that the inability to express yourself clearly and effectively in every one of the above examples can prevent you from achieving your goal.

Pastoral Calm

A PARABLE OF FEW WORDS:

"I pointed out the moon to you . . . and all you saw was my finger." (Swahili Proverb)

INDONESIA: BALI

A T A GLANCE   BALI

Population: *2,500,000*
Language: *Indonesian*
Literacy: *64%*
Faith: *Bali-Hinduism*
Currency: *Rupiah*

POSTCARD
REFLECTIONS

Actually felt a bit sluggish (like a pooped water buffalo!) after gala birthday party for Jesus. Three strolling Bali guitarists climaxed the festivities at our table singing: Cuando Calient'el Sol, Besame Mucho, I Left My Heart In You-Know-Where, I Just Called To Say I Love You— and other Christmas favorites.

Prepared for a solemn high celebration of Christmas. . . Bali High.

No, it was not so difficult celebrating my 25th anniversary and Jesus' birthday so far from home, it just made me miss my family and friends more.

This wonderful old Balinese woman preparing Betel for chewing became my Christmas card. I sent several hundred to friends and family in the United States — wishing them Christmas blessings .

SMILES to go

In a cocktail lounge:

> Ladies are requested not to have children in the bar.

FR. NORBERT SHADEG, S.V.D: devout missionary and superb communicator who has so mastered the local language and cultural communication that he is one of Bali's most famous published semanticists.

Dancing warrior simulates suicide during the famous and traditional Barong Kris Dance.

I want you to meet some of my Bali friends . . . celebrated Christmas together this year . . .

FACES OF BALI

149

INDONESIA: BALI

Bali

CREATIVE
COMMUNICATING

In Bali the Wayang Shadow Puppet Plays teach their
Hindu Dharma religion (95% of the Balinese)—belief in:

BRAHMAN: One God
ATMAN: Soul and Spirit
SAMSARA: Reincarnation
KARMA: Reciprocity
MOKSHA: Nirvana.

"Tat Twan Asi" = "You are as I am."

They have perfected a new creative form of medium
for religious communication!

On Christmas day it rained— I
didn't let that keep me from the
pool at the Diwangkara (sunshine)
bungalows pool.

I was blessed to celebrate two "midnight Masses" on Christmas eve: the first at 9 p.m. on the 10th floor of the Bali Beach Hotel and the second at 11 p.m. on the white moonlit sands of the Bali Hyatt, where a torrential rain storm interrupted my sermon. Merry Christmas.

PARABLE OF THE GIFT

Persons are gifts sent to me wrapped! Some are wrapped very beautifully; they are attractive when I first see them. Many come in very ordinary wrapping paper. Others have been mishandled in the mail. Once in a while there is a "special delivery." Persons are sometimes gifts that come very loosely wrapped, others very tightly.

But the wrapping is not the gift! It is easy to make that mistake. Some of the gifts are very easy to open up. On other occasions I need others to help. Is it because they are afraid? Does it hurt? Maybe they have been opened up before and thrown away!

I am a person. Therefore, I am a gift, too, a gift to myself first of all. Have I ever looked inside the wrappings? Afraid to? Perhaps I've never accepted the gift that I am. How can I be a gift to others until I realize that I myself am a gift from God.

Every meeting of persons should be an exchange of gifts. But a gift without a giver is not a gift.

PHILIPPINES

AT A GLANCE   **PHILIPPINES**

Population: 61,971,000
Capital With Population: Manila 1,700,000
Language: Filipino, English, Spanish
Literacy: 88%
Faith Expression: Roman Catholic (83%),
          Protestant (9%), Islam (7%)
Currency used: Philippine peso
Cities I Visited: Manila

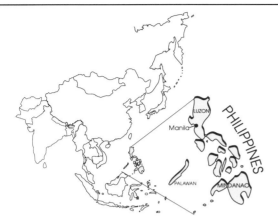

How often during my year's pilgrimage what at first seemed bad news had turned to good news. For example, late one night on a train in West Germany I was harshly arrested and taken to the police station. It was a mistake and I was released. But that experience helped prepare me for all the gratuitous imprisonments Catholic priests, sisters and teachers suffer all over the developing world when they challenge their unjust governments.

My involvement in both a car accident and a boating tragedy in East Africa turned into teachable moments. "Interminal" waiting for planes, trains and buses—including two and a half days at a West African airport—provided opportunities to get to know people I otherwise would never have met. Being denied entry into Burma and Sri Lanka added valuable time in Thailand and Singapore. Once my baggage was lost, three times things were stolen: maddening but good lessons in detachment. Language barriers taught humility and humor. In Seoul, Korea, where no one spoke English, I had to speak Italian to my Rome-trained host, and he translated into Korean for the 27 priests I was teaching. What I thought would be the worst experiences of all—being alone for both my silver jubilee and Christmas—became moments of grace and closeness to Christ.

How often our crises lead to opportunities, our crosses to resurrections, our loneliness to love. God knows better than we do who we are and what we need—which brings me to this story.

PARABLE OF THE WISE FARMER

An old farmer had an old horse for tilling his fields. One day the horse escaped into the hills. When all the farmer's neighbors sympathized with the old man over his bad luck, the farmer replied, "Bad luck? Good luck? Who knows?"

A week later the horse returned with a herd of wild horses from the hills. And this time the neighbors congratulated the farmer on his good luck. His reply was: "Good luck? Bad luck? Who knows?"

Then, when the farmer's son was attempting to tame one of the wild horses, he fell off its back and broke his leg. Everyone thought this very bad luck. Not the farmer, whose only reaction was: "Bad luck? Good luck? Who knows?"

Some weeks later the army marched into the village and conscripted every able-bodied youth they found there. When they saw the farmer's son with his broken leg, they let him off. Good luck? Bad luck? Who knows?

Everything that seems on the surface to be evil may be a good in disguise. And everything that seems good on the surface may really be an evil. So we are wise when we leave it to God to decide what is good and what bad and thank Him that all things turn out for good with those who love Him.

In a tailor shop:

> Order your summers suit. Because in big rush we will execute customers in strict rotation.

Smiles to go

Fr. Jean Desautels and Fr. Jim Reuter

PARABLE OF ENLIGHTENMENT

A Chinese peasant called Chung-Fu led a simple life selling fish in the marketplace. As he advanced in age, however, he felt the need for spiritual enlightenment. He decided to approach a master whom he knew well, who had lived in his own village and had retired to a cave where he meditated and enlightened inquirers. Chung-Fu went to him, renewed his acquaintance and asked for advice in the search he wanted to undertake for his true self and his new life.

"Help me to find out who I am," he asked, "and what I am supposed to do." The master, who knew him well and knew his life, looked at him intently and uttered these profound words of guidance: "You are Chung-Fu and you are supposed to sell fish in the marketplace."

I'm Miles Riley. I'm supposed to communicate the Good News in the marketplace—or, as my Master puts it, "to the ends of the earth." And I love it.

PHILIPPINES

Letter from Manila

CREATIVE
COMMUNICATING

Miles!

Pax Christi.

It was amazing!... The same kind of questions you asked in the ambush interviews!

Then the same Bishops, whom you taught, met together and got out the strongest statement the Church has issued against any government since the days of Henry the Eighth of England.

Our timing was right.

The revolution itself was as joyous as a town fiesta. We stopped the tanks, and the soldiers, with people. The people were not only men. They were women, children, teenagers, babies, boys and girls. They did it with flowers, with laughter, with coffee and sandwiches, with prayer, with the rosary, and with incredible courage.

Cardinal Sin believes that the Virgin Mary, personally, ran the revolution. Her statue was on the top of the guardhouse, in the center of the main gate of Camp Aguinaldo. Her statue was carried behind Enrile and Ramos, wherever they went. When the people were pressed, they were praying the rosary. It was really a landmark in the history of the world.

The channel that carried the satellite telecasts from the Vatican in 1985—both at Easter and at Christmas—was Channel 4. This is where all the action was, during the revolution! Enrile and Ramos took Channel 4 on Monday morning. Marcos left on Tuesday night. From noon on Monday until midnight on Tuesday, the people were in the streets around the television station, to meet the tanks and the troops. All those who were broadcasting knew that they could be killed at any moment.

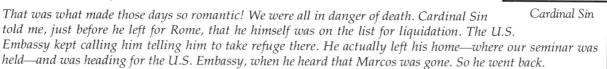

Cardinal Sin

That was what made those days so romantic! We were all in danger of death. Cardinal Sin told me, just before he left for Rome, that he himself was on the list for liquidation. The U.S. Embassy kept calling him telling him to take refuge there. He actually left his home—where our seminar was held—and was heading for the U.S. Embassy, when he heard that Marcos was gone. So he went back.

Please pray for us here. We need it here!

Hopefully,

Jim Reuter, S.J.

PARABLE OF THE STONE

Diogenes was standing at a street corner one day laughing like a man out of his mind.

"What are you laughing about?" a passerby asked.

"Do you see that stone in the middle of the street? Since I got here this morning ten people have stumbled on it and cursed it. But not one of them took the trouble to remove it so others wouldn't stumble."

It is now history: the peaceful peoples' revolution removed the stone, the scandalum of the Marcos regime. The two weapons which the world considers most powerful, money and military might, were defeated by faith and communication.

Cardinal Vidal communicates with Papal Nuncio Archbishop Bruno Torpigliani.

Enrolling over 200 teachers in one of our full day communication workshops.

(left to right) Fr. Anthony Scanell, O.F.M., Director of the Franciscan Communications Center in Los Angeles and President of UNDA World; Bishop Agnellus Andrew, founder of Catholic Radio and Television Training Center in Hatch End, London; Archbishop John Foley, President of the Pontifical Commission for Social Communication at the Vatican; and the author . . .

Fr. Pat Peyton ("The family that prays together stays together") greets Archbishop Foley.

OCEANIA

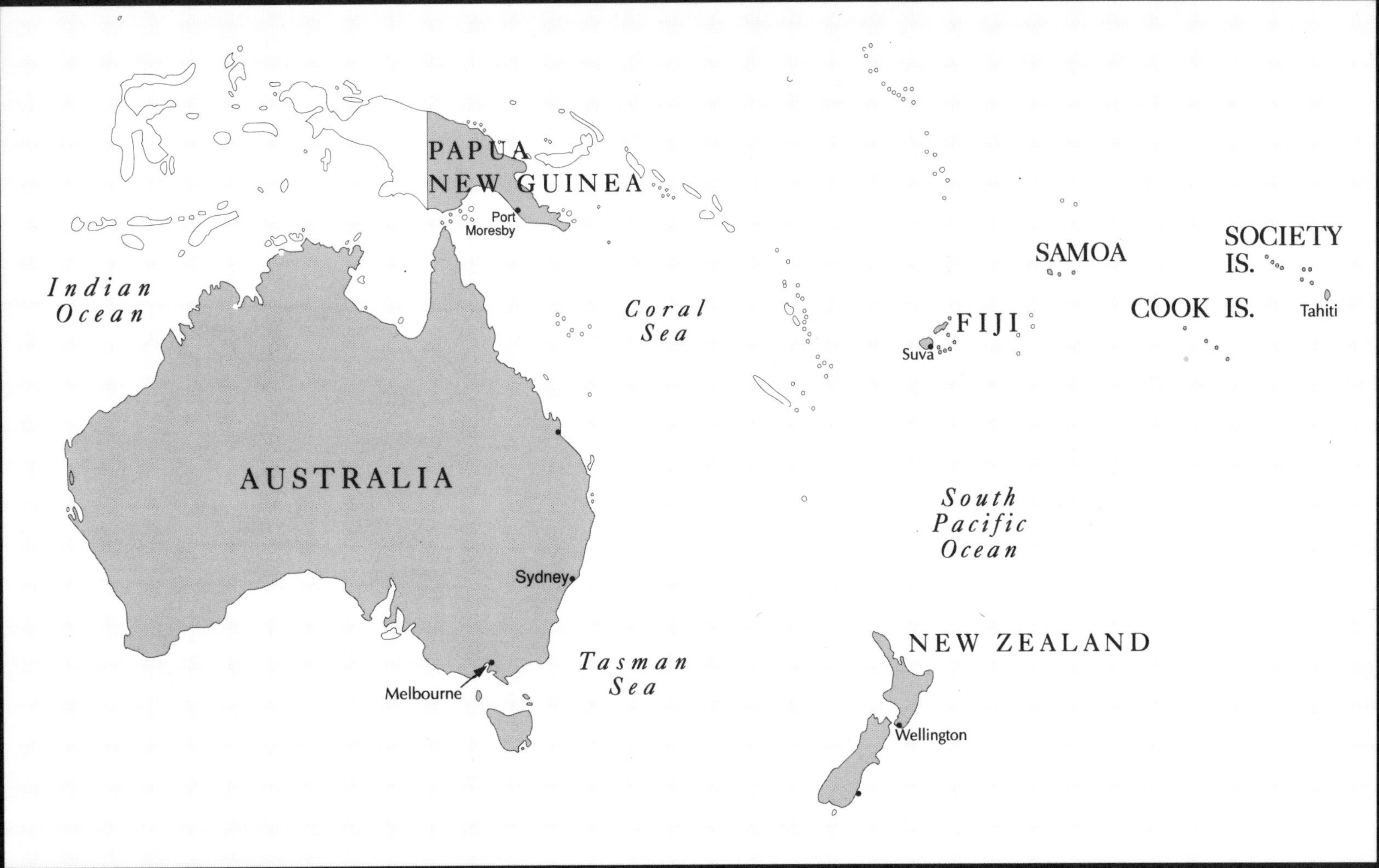

SOCIETY IS.

Tahiti

COOK IS.

SAMOA

FIJI

Suva

South
Pacific
Ocean

NEW ZEALAND

Wellington

Coral
Sea

Tasman
Sea

PAPUA
NEW GUINEA

Port
Moresby

Sydney

AUSTRALIA

Melbourne

Indian
Ocean

SAMOA

A T A GLANCE   SAMOA
Population: 200,000
Capital With Population: Apia 34,000
Language: Samoan, English
Literacy: 90%
Faith Expression: Protestant (75%), Roman Catholic (22%)
Currency Used: Tala
Cities I Visited: Apia

SAMOA

In the background is downtown Apia: Twin Towers belong to the cathedral where we stayed. 20 countries from South Pacific attended this conference. I taught TV production. Samoans are beautiful, simple, gentle—with proud culture and traditions.

Mulivai Cathedral

Smiles to go

In a laundry:

Ladies, leave your clothes here and spend the afternoon having a good time.

KEY SAMOAN PHRASES

Hello.	**Talofa**
Good-bye.	**Tofa**
I want to eat.	**Ua 'ou fia ai**
I want to swim in the sea.	**Ou te fia ta'ele i le sami**
Do you want to dance?	**E te fia siva?**
No, thank you.	**Leai faafetai**

CARDINAL PIO TAOFINU'U: the singing, dancing, loving, communicating Cardinal would lead us in prayer, pour cocktails, wait on table during meals, wash the dishes and lead the traditional folk dances after dinner. A respected leader in the Samoan community, Cardinal Pio is building a media center with AV studios to enlarge and enhance the Church's ministry in the islands.

PESAMINO VICTOR: kind, caring family man—for Samoans the family is everything—husband/father of his love family in the village and quiet leader of his faith family in the church. Pesamino also takes a team approach to communications: producing invocations (10-minute devotional sign-on programs) and benedictions (midnight scriptural meditations) for the local radio station . . . also produces audio cassette recordings of Renew songs—distributed with booklet.

159

SAMOA

MICRONESIA

SR. CARMEN DASKO WILLIAMS:
strong and gentle, quiet and articulate, a team player with leadership talent—another of the take-charge women who are beginning to lead the countries and communities of our global village to peace.

KIRIBATI

SR. TENETI BAKAREREUA:
youthful, genuine, dedicated, with a flair for the creative and the business-like methodology to put imaginative, people-ideas into practice.

SOLOMON ISLANDS

FR. JAN GIESSELINK:
gifted ideographer and committed communicator who is not intimidated by technology and is comfortable with the creative challenges of the mass media ministry.

IDEAS IN MEDIA MINISTRY

CREATIVE
COMMUNICATING

To give you an idea of some of the creative communicating taking place in Oceania, here is a list of projects funded by UNDA-OCIC for 1989–1990 in some of the 13 countries represented at the UNDA-OCIC continental conference in Apia, Samoa.

- **UNDA** Oceania Regional Programs: $13,250

- **Papua New Guinea Communication Institute** Religious Radio Production: $13,480

- **Pacific Islands CEPAC** Support for Training Program: $2,941

- **Carolines/Marshalls: Diocese** Local Training in Production Skills, Media Education: $1,573

- **Carolines/Marshalls: Truk State** Purchase of Production Equipment: $1,409

- **Kiribati Diocese** Radio Production Costs: $3,863

- **Solomon Islands** Video Equipment Purchase and Maintenance: $7,000

- **Pacific Islands Regional Seminary** Continue Upgrading Training Studio: $963

- **Cook Islands Diocese** Soundproofing of Studio Air Time: $4,250

- **Papua New Guinea Bougainville Diocese** Security of Production Equipment: $1,500

- **American Samoa Diocese** Radio and Television Air Time: $4,400

- **Wallis and Futuna** Local Video Library: not specified

- **Western Samoa Archdiocese** Equipment for Radio Production: $11,500

- **Western Samoa Faleata and Si'usega Parishes** Video Production for Catechists: $9,470

ST. PAUL'S STUDIO, KIRIBATI

Radio Programs

There are three main programs allowed to all churches by Radio Kiribati:

1. Sunday Mass or services for 45 minutes at 12 noon every fortnight

2. Sunday Scriptures for 15 minutes at 8:45 pm every fortnight

3. 5-minute morning devotions at 6:30 from Monday to Saturday every three weeks

4. Special programs for special events for half-hour or more, only if wanted.

We pay for all these programs to the radio station. ($1/min!)

Three sisters are working full time at St. Paul's Studio. They are Sisters Beneteta, Otina and Teneti. They are working together as a team. Their main work is to produce radio programs from beginning to end. "The main purposes are to spread the Good News to our own people and to meet our expenses for Broadcasting Fees.

"For the first time, I changed our 15 minutes Sunday programmes into a *Radio Magazine Programme*. The people like this kind of programme very much, because they can hear the Church news, stories of our early Missionaries, new songs and hymns and help from the Bible at the end."

PARABLE OF YOUR BEAUTY

"Why is everyone here so happy except me?"

"Because they have learned to see goodness and beauty everywhere," said the Master.

"Why don't I see goodness and beauty everywhere?"

"Because you cannot see outside of you what you fail to see inside."

NEW ZEALAND

A T A GLANCE   **NEW ZEALAND**

Population: 3,397,000
Capital With Population: Wellington 587,700
Language: English, Maori
Literacy: 99.5%
Faith Expression: Prostestant, Anglican (29%),
       Presbyterian (18%), Roman Catholic (15%),
       Others
Currency Used: New Zealand dollar

POSTCARD
R E F L E C T I O N S

From time to time, in this life, you gotta stop in New Zealand and smell the flowers.

Four days in Wellington and two days in Christ's Church. Chilly dead of winter here down under! Loved the 3 million people but did not meet all 70,000 sheep.

On the box of a clockwork toy:

Guaranteed to work throughout its useful life.

Smiles to go

The city of Wellington

Port Nicholson boat harbor, Wellington

FR. JAMES B. LYONS: creative, centered communications director of National Media office of New Zealand Catholic Bishops'Conference; provides excellent public relations (has mastered the art of creating and placing stories—of getting the Good News on the evening news), an Annual Catholic Directory, a network of diocesan directors of communication, training and production of at least one super video a year. During the last seven years they have created a 1/2 hour video on a different sacrament each year.

CARDINAL THOMAS WILLIAMS: strong leader, sympathetic communicator with a special concern for the Maori people and social justice.

SR. ELIZABETH RUSSELL, S.J.C.: intelligent, warm, classy classic example of what happens in Catholic communications the world over.

The most gifted church people are called or drawn to the media ministry and then because of their obvious talents, asked to contribute to other educational and evangelical apostolates.

NEW ZEALAND

CREATIVE
COMMUNICATING

IDEAS IN MEDIA MINISTRY

In order to publish and publicize the bishops' pastoral statements, The National Catholic Communications Office produces little booklets or brochures which are clean, simple, clear and artistic. The colorful cover of their 1990 statement on the justice due the Maori (original New Zealanders) begins:

Tihei mauri ora.
Ka poua te Pou tuatahi Ko te Ao me ona mea katoa;
Ka poua te Pou tuarua
Ko te Tangata hei kaitiaki mo te Ao;
Ko Tama-nui o te Ao katoa; He Atua! He Tangata!
Whano! Whano! Tu mai te Ripeka!
Haumi e! Hui e e e! Taiki e!

Behold, we live.
Life has three signposts
— the world, and all living things
— the people, guardians of the world
— the divine and human Son, the Saviour;
Come!
Let us go to the Cross standing before us.
Let us bind together in solidarity.

THE EVENING POST, WELLINGTON, NEW ZEALAND JUNE 8, 1988:

Fr. Riley finding ways to serve

He is in New Zealand for six days as part of a 51-country trip, learning what other countries are doing in Catholic communication.

'Radio and television broadcasts might not be the best way to communicate religion,' he said. 'Are there any conversions from this? Are we better off with videos or cassettes for the car?' There was no simple answer to better communicating the 2000 year-old Christian message, 'We have to find new language for old truths. The answer is not in our heads but in our hearts; the God stories of our own experience—the personal story of faith.'

Fr. Miles O'Brien Riley — looking at ways of being "our brother's brother".

PARABLE OF THE STATUES

To a pioneering spirit who was discouraged by frequent criticism the Master said, "Listen to the words of the critic. He reveals what your friends hide from you."

But he also said, "Do not be weighed down by what the critic says. No statue was ever erected to honor a critic. Statues are for the criticized."

AUSTRALIA: MELBOURNE *A*

T A GLANCE **AUSTRALIA**
Population: *16,500,000*
Capital With Population: *Canberra, 282,000;
    Melbourne, Victoria 4,188,300*
Language: *English, aboriginal languages*
Literacy: *99%*
Faith Expression: *Anglican 26%, (15% practicing)
    Protestant 25%, Roman Catholic 27%
    (15% practicing)*
Currency Used: *Australian dollar*

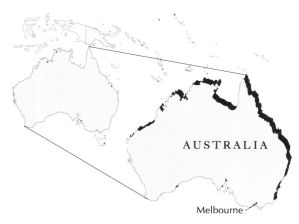

POSTCARD
REFLECTIONS

Only 6 folks in Melbourne's workshop—but it went very well. Had informative and constructive dinner with the Archbishop. Enjoyed quality communication time with local Cardinals and Bishops.

At a zoo:

Please do not feed the animals. If you have any suitable food, give it to the guard on duty.

Which way to the church?

You're in it.

AUSTRALIA: MELBOURNE

CATHOLIC COMMUNICATIONS CENTER

CREATIVE
COMMUNICATING

R adio Productions

Crossways — a religious, current affairs format with an emphasis on the model of a Christian presence of service. 1 hour/weekly. 3AW, 9 PM Sunday.

Voices of Our World — (Produced in the U.S.) Actuality material gathered from 30 countries of people, 'Calling for a better world'. 30 minutes/weekly. 3RPH, 5.30 pm Sunday.

God's People — a radio liturgy produced for radio for the print handicapped. 2 x 30 minutes/weekly. 3RPH, 9.30 am and 3.00 pm Sunday.

Connections — an ecumenical news/magazine format produced for the print handicapped. 30 minutes weekly. 3RPH, 8.30 pm Thursday.

Tapestry — a music and talk format featuring top 40 tracks and young people expressing their opinions about a variety of issues. 1 hour/weekly. 3FOX-FM, 10.30 pm Sunday.

Spots — variety of 'home grown' and other spots distributed to several stations. 3AK, 3EON-FM, 3KZ, 3GL, 3MP.

Family Counsellor — a 'talk-back' counselling programme with the back-up resources of a major welfare (Associated Programme) agency. 4 hours/weekly. 3DB, 8 pm. Sunday.

T elevision Productions

Sunday Magazine — a magazine, news format programme which vigorously promotes human dignity and a sense of justice and willingness to share with those most in need. 30 minutes/weekly. HSV7, 8.30 am. Sunday.

Mass For You At Home — a televised eucharist shot in close-up. The 'president' relates to the viewers as congregation. 30 minutes/weekly. ATV10, 8.30 Sunday.

Footprints — a children's programme, presented by children, produced in Brisbane. 30 minutes/28 per annum. GTV 9, 7.30 am Sunday.

Insight — (produced in the U.S.) dramatic presentations of life issues. 30 minutes/weekly. HSV7, After late movie, Sunday.

Special Documentaries — high budget productions which, although primarily made for television, are distributed as video resources. 30/40 minutes/4 per annum.

Telespots — 30 and 60 second spots. GTV9, Scattered, all time zones.

CATHOLIC COMMUNICATIONS CENTER

Mission Statement

To communicate through mass media authentically human values as lived by Jesus and witnessed to in the traditions and teachings of the Church.

The theological problem today is to find the art of drawing religion out of people, not pumping it into them. The redemption has happened. The holy spirit is in people . . . and the art is to help people become what they are.

Karl Rahner

PARABLE FOR FINDING GOD

"What action shall I perform to attain God?"

"If you wish to attain God, there are two things you must know.

The first is that all efforts to attain God are of no avail."

"And the second?"

"You must act as if you did not know the first."

Australia: Sydney

A T A GLANCE   AUSTRALIA
Population: 16,500,000
Capital With Population: Canberra, 282,000;
        Melbourne, Victoria 4,188,300
Language: English, aboriginal languages
Literacy: 99%
Faith Expression: Anglican 26%, (15% practicing)
        Protestant 25%, Roman Catholic 27%
        (15% practicing)
Currency Used: Australian dollar

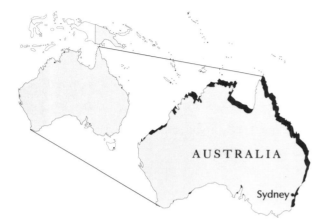

Using the media as well as teaching the media here in Australia . . . Radio/TV/Newspapers. What fun to be in a country once again where English is the 1st language . . . sort of.

POSTCARD
REFLECTIONS

Good Lord, Mate, not another postcard to 441 Church St.!

You may recognize me from my TV appearances . . . tho' I try never to speak for my country with my mouth full!

SR. MARGARET LE BRETON: I remember the first time I met Sr. Margie. She and Josie (cute, bubbly, efficient office manager) were waiting in ambush for me at Jim McLaren's "Crosswalk Productions." They had decorated the entrance hall with multicolorful welcoming signs and a huge poster with a fabulous long poem in "Aussie jargonese" personally greeting me. They made me feel like a rock star or celebrity athlete. And then there was this lovely quiet religious woman with an intoxicating smile on her lips and a microphone in her hand. "Welcome to Australia. May we do a little radio interview on death and resurrection for our network Easter special?" You don't say 'no' to Sr. Margie. Her charm and gentle kindness, combined with a strong background in youth work and religious formation make her a wonderful producer.

Sidney ear specialist diagnosed trauma of inner canals from 60 flights in 9 months! Have now seen 4 docs in 4 weeks, am taking drops for ears, drops for nose, pills for mouth and 2 inhalants and I'm grounded for a week—while I learn to read lips and sign language . . . or clear me ears!

Peek-a-boo!

I Love Kangaroos

with Fr. Jim McClaren, Sr. Margie and Josie

171

Australia: Sydney

FR. JAMES MCLAREN:
Affectionately referred to as "The Voice" because of his deep, resonant baritone which is familiar to the radio listeners of New South Wales where Fr. Jim has been hosting call-in radio shows for many years. Fr. Jim is also founding director of "Crosswalk Productions" ("programmes with a conscience") a distribution network of radio spots, series and specials syndicated throughout Australian radio. At present, Fr. Jim is serving as chairman and CEO of "2 SM" (Two SM) the Catholic Church's own radio station in Sydney which is undergoing radical changes (conversions?) in personnel and format—from "lite and easy" to "adult contemporary." He is also administrating St. Mark's Parish in Sydney—and providing magic, marvelous hospitality for traveling priest-communicators. But what Fr. Jim is best and most is a friend.

FR. KEVIN BURTON:
grand gentleman of Catholic communications in Australia and spiritual "grandfather" (along with Fr. Pat Casserly of Fiji) of many media missionaries in the South Pacific, director of Sydney's Catholic Communications Center, and perhaps the one individual on my entire global pilgrimage who most deserves the title: "host with the most." I cannot remember how many times Kevin met or delivered me to the airport in Sydney—I stopped in Sydney 6 times on my way to and from Asia, Oceania, and Africa (it

CREATIVE
COMMUNICATING

Crosswalk Productions

Programmes with a conscience—a creative production center for Catholic spiritual radio programming: spots, series and seasonal specials which are recorded in Sydney and then syndicated to many radio stations throughout Australia. Fr. Jim McLaren, Sr. Margie and Josie who run "Crosswalk" offer quarterly "packages" of radio programming to subscribing stations at an annual rate.

Catholic Communications Center

The Catholic Communications Center in Sydney does a simple bit of communicating that most broadcast AV communicators forget to do: they publish a little four-page monthly newsletter—with photos, short articles, announcements, educational pieces, requests for support, etc.—to build up their own 'communications family' and keep them informed and connected . . . little things mean a lot.

COMMUNICATION

Vol. 20 No. 2   CATHOLIC COMMUNICATIONS CENTRE, SYDNEY   FEBRUARY, 1989

Registered by Australia Post — Publication No. NAR0604

U.S. BROADCASTER IN SYDNEY

Miles O'Brien Riley is a broadcaster with a difference. He's a Catholic priest from San Francisco where he heads up the Archdiocese Communications Office. He also holds doctorate degrees in theology (Gregorian University, Rome) and Communications (University of California). But he's no mere theoretical academic. Since 1970 Fr. Miles' main ministry has been the mass media. He has written five musical comedies, nine books and hundreds of articles and reviews. He has produced and hosted eight films and over 1000 television and 3000 radio programs. He is on radio and TV daily in Northern California.

Fr. Miles is a personalised communications dynamo. On a recent visit to Sydney, hosted by the Catholic Communications Centre, he exhibited his many talents as a communicator for God. Interviewed on 2BL by Andrew Olle, Miles O'Brien Riley quickly established both his superb professionalism as a radio communicator and his ability as a public representative of Christ as well as the disarming warmth and humour of his personality.

Unconventional in many ways Fr. Miles O'Brien Riley nevertheless left no doubt in anyone's mind where he stood on many fundamental issues. Whether addressing his colleagues, being interviewed by the media or in the course of his strict daily regimen of physical exercise he made it clear that here was a man completely given to Christ, the Church and the priesthood — a man totally committed to truth.

He is a man with a mission — to tell the world of the love of Christ — a man who sees all human convention as an extension of that love in all his meetings with the people whether on a one-to-one basis or through the media.

Sydney was fortunate to have been touched, however briefly, by Fr. Miles O'Brien Riley.

PARABLE OF LIGHT

The Master had been on his deathbed in a coma for weeks. One day he suddenly opened his eyes to find his favorite disciple there.

"You never leave my bedside, do you?" he said softly.

"No, Master. I cannot."

"Why?"

"Because you are the light of my life."

The Master sighed. "Have I so dazzled you, my son, that you still refuse to see the light in you?"

FIJI

AT A GLANCE   **FIJI**
Population: 758,000
Capital With Population: Suva 75,000
Language: English, Fijian, Hindustani
Literacy: 86%
Faith Expression: Christian 52%, Hindu 40%,
        Moslem 8%
Currency Used: Fijian dollar

FIJI

Suva

God in the Tropics!

fiji

SUVA
9 AM
30 JAN
1989

POSTCARD
REFLECTIONS

Getting the clothes washed was one of the major challenges of this trip!

Toyota!

174

CREATIVE COMMUNICATING

Communications pioneer of the South Pacific, Fr. Pat Casserly set up the important training center in Papua New Guinea and then moved to Suva, Fiji, to serve as media consultant to the Bishop's Conference of Oceania and set up another training and production center in audio and video at the Marist Seminary in Suva, Fiji—so close to the gorgeous ocean that students can videotape passing ships and audio record the soft breezes as they learn new creative methods for presenting the good news of God's loving presence in all of creation. It was a pleasure to live and work with Fr. Pat for a week (his balcony by the bay remains—with Fort Aguada in Goa and La Paz, Bolivia—one of the exquisite views on planet Earth!) exploring ways to make up the lack of a big budget with careful preparation, thoughtful scripture, and innovative approaches to production.

PROFILES
Creative Communicators

FR. PAT CASSERLY, S.M.: scholarly, urbane, not afraid to get his hands dirty shooting video or editing audio, Fr. Pat serves as media consultant for CEPAC, the Bishops' Conference of the South Pacific and teaches practical audio and video production at the Marist Seminary in Suva.

PIO CAKAU: humble man of faith and hope and humor—a good example of the laborers of love who keep Catholic Communication alive around the world—Pio is especially proud of their radio broadcasts of the Mass—and morning devotionals and thought-probing spots.

PARABLE OF THE SEARCH

A man asked the guru to take him on as a disciple.

If what you seek is truth," said the guru, "there are requirements to be fulfilled and duties to be discharged."

"What are these?"

"You will have to draw water and chop wood and do the housecleaning and cooking."

"I am in search of Truth, not employment," said the man, as he walked away.

The "Christian Family Video Society of Fiji" has obtained $40–50,000 in grants to build up its video cassette library of several hundred great titles—from popular Hollywood feature movies to specifically religious educational videos.

PAPUA NEW GUINEA

A T A GLANCE   *PAPUA NEW GUINEA*
Population: *3,613,000*
Capital with population: *Port Moresby 152,000*
Language: *English and local languages*
Faith: *Animist, Protestant, 63%, Roman Catholic 31%*
Currency: *Kina*
City visited: *Port Moresby, Goroka*

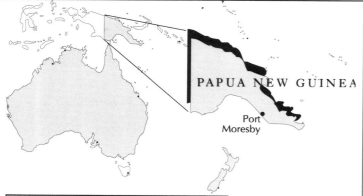

The toughest weather and most rugged people are found along the Papua New Guinea coast—where nature is in charge, though usually benevolent and provident . . . 700 different tribal cultures communicate with one another in pidgin: a mix of English, Australian (!), German and God only knows how many different dialect polyglot!

POSTCARD REFLECTIONS

Papua New Guinea

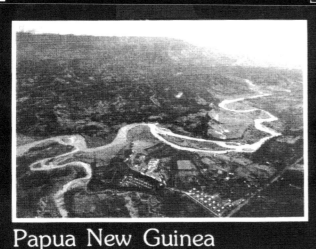

Papua New Guinea

This was my first—and last—overview of Papua New Guinea, from the small jet flying between Port Moresby on the southern coast up to Goroka, at 3000 feet in the N-E highlands. It will probably remain as my lasting impression or memory . . . but did I love those Goroka mountains, waking up in the early morning mist from under their warm quilted blankets of clouds.

SMILES to go

The Gods must be crazy!

At the market . . .

Mealtime for Sr. Mary and Fr. Miles

CHARLES BASSE:
young talented local professional videographer who has made the Communications Institute his work and religious communicating his ministry. There are a number of local staff people—recently enriched by the arrival of talented church communicator Fr. Jan Giesselink, S.M.—who really operate as a team. I hope they will understand if I let Charles, his talent, dedication and smiling energy represent all of them.

SR. MARY HUDSON:
the guiding head and heart behind (in front of!) C.I.'s extraordinary productivity and successful service. Sr. Mary is the kind of leader who brings out the best in others, who trusts and delegates and supports— and knows how to play and pray: two ingredients at the foundation of any effective communications enterprise. I believe that the key to Sr. Mary's and C.I.'s success is the daily mass that the entire staff celebrate at the altar of the Lord early each morning. Close to Christ, they are able to communicate the message—and the MESSENGER!

PAPUA NEW GUINEA

Media for Human Development
COMMUNICATION INSTITUTE
P.O. Box 448, Goroka, E.H.P. Papua New Guinea
Telephone: 72 1117

CREATIVE
COMMUNICATING

The Communication Institute

The Communication Institute in Papua, New Guinea is one of the great training centers in the Developing World. Here are some practical examples of both their production and training activities the year I visited—and taught a week long radio course to 12 apostles from all over the South Pacific.

1.   Production

1.1   Radio programmes (Pidgin or English)

Regular programmes sent to N.B.C. National and Provincial Stations:
- Input 5 mins. 3 × fortnightly
- News/nius 15 mins. monthly
- Lotu bilong Wailis/Church of the Air. 30 mins. monthly

Special half hour programmes are produced for New Year, Good Friday, Easter and Christmas. Documentaries of 30 to 45 mins. are produced on request from NBC Religious Department.

1.2   Audio Cassettes

New productions for 1989:
- "Ave Maria" a Marian year special. English hymns.
- "Litimapim Nem bilong God". Pidgin songs.
- Educational cassettes "Stories of long ago" "Stori bilong ol tumbuna" are in progress.

1.3   Video

A series on the sacraments and the psalms have been planned. Ordinations and profession ceremonies have been taped.

1.4   Media Education

A kit "Photolanguage PNG" featuring 98 different pictures of people and life in P.N.G. has been assembled and made available.

2. Training

Topics	Participants
Techniques of broadcasting	6 trainees from PNG and Solomons
Group Media, Public Relations	Deacons, Bomana
Appearing on Television	Bishops and Church Leaders
Introduction to Mass Media	Sisters in Formation Xavier Institute
Group Media and Intro. to Mass Media	E.H.P. Urban Youth Coordinators. Goroka
Foundations of Communication and Media Ed.	
for Health Workers.	Highlands Provincial Nutritionists, Goroka
Media Education	High School Teachers
Media in service kit	Curriculum Division Education Department
	Port Moresby
Photolanguage and Photojournalism	Divine Word Institute Communication Arts Students
	Madang
Foundations of Communication and Intro. to Mass Media	St. Fidelis College Kap. Madang
Story telling techniques for Media	Communication Arts students. D.W.I. Madang
Communication Techniques for Health	Provincial Nutritionists Madang
Personality Integration	Goroka Teachers' College. Psychology Students
Self and others (PRH)	Nurses - St. Joseph's Medical Centre Mingende
Dynamics of Communication (PRH)	Students. Christian Formation Centre Mingende
Wokim Video	Open Course
Media Education for Pastoral Workers	Novices - Holy Spirit Sisters Madang

Teaching radio production to religious representatives from various South Pacific islands.

PAPUA NEW GUINEA

O f Global Interest . . .The following information is taken from the Catholic Media Council Information Bulletin (and C.I. News Sept. '89)

Christian Radio Stations in Developing Countries

	Cath.	Prot.
CARIBBEAN:		
Anguilla		1
Antigua		1
Dominica	1	1
Guadeloupe	1	
Haiti	3	1
Martinique	1	
Netherlands Antilles		1
Puerto Rico	1	6
Republica Dominicana	5	
St. Kitts - Nevis		1
Turks and Caicos Islands		1
Virgin Islands		1
total	**12**	**14**
LATIN AMERICA		
Argentina	4	
Bolivia	19	2
Brazil	121	8
Chile	10	2
Colombia	12	1
Costa Rica	7	2

(+ ICER Instituto Costaricense de Enseñanza Radiofonica. FM network with about 16 stations)

	Cath.	Prot.
Ecuador	22	5
El Salvador	4	1
Guatemala	12	3
Honduras	7	1
Mexico	3	1
Nicaragua	2	1
Panama	2	2
Peru	19	2
Uruguay	1	
Venezuela	6	
total	**252**	**32**

	Cath.	Prot.
SOUTH PACIFIC		
Guam		1
ASIA		
Indonesia	9	1

The Catholic Communication Centre Sanggar Prathivi produces weekly radio programmes for 120 radio stations throughout the country.

	Cath.	Prot.
Philippines	22	4

Since 1988 a rapid extension of the Catholic radio ministry is strongly promoted: 18 new diocesan stations are going to be established and 11 others are planned.

	Cath.	Prot.
South Korea	1	3

Actually a Catholic radio station in the diocese of Kwangju is in preparation.

	Cath.	Prot.
Sri Lanka		1
Taiwan	2	
total	**34**	**9**
AFRICA		
Liberia	2	1
Seychelles		1
Swaziland		1
Zaire	3	
total	**5**	**3**

Pending projects in the Catholic Church (under consideration):

IVORY COAST: Radio 10 Montagnes
LIBERIA: Extension of Radio ECLM to a regional station for West Africa;
BOTSWANA/LESOTHO/BOTSWANA: establishment of a regional station for Southern Africa.

PARABLE OF THE LITTLE FISH

Once upon a time, there was a little fish. When he was young his mother often told him about the big beautiful ocean that one day he would discover for himself.

When the little fish was old enough and strong enough, he set off on his journey to find the Ocean. He swam and swam and searched everywhere for that magnificent Ocean.

One day, he met a big fish. He thought to himself: "Big fish—he must have lived a long time. He will know where to find the Ocean."

"Good morning, Big Fish."

"Good morning, Little Fish."

"Excuse me, Big Fish, but I am trying to find the Ocean . . . Can you direct me to the Ocean?"

"Little Fish, this is the Ocean—you're in it!"

"Oh no, Big Fish, this is only water!"

The Big Fish swam away sadly, saying to himself: "How do you tell a little fish about the mystery of the Ocean?"

COOK IS.

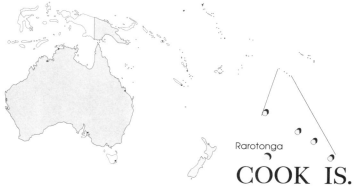

Rarotonga

COOK IS.

This is our city on our island. I've climbed that mountain once— Sir Edmund Hilary, eat your heart out!

POSTCARD
REFLECTIONS

Consider the postage stamp: it's usefulness consists in the ability to stick to one thing, till it gets there

Josh Billings

I have been considering these little sticky devils for months! If only I had a quarter for every stamp I licked during my year's pilgrimage!

PARABLE OF THE RIVER

As the Master grew old and infirm, the disciples begged him not to die. Said the Master, "If I did not go, how would you ever see?"

"What is it we fail to see when you are with us?" they asked.

But the Master would not say.

When the moment of his death was near, they said, "What is it we will see when you are gone?"

With a twinkle in his eye, the Master said, "All I did was sit on the riverbank handing out river water. After I'm gone, I trust you will notice the river."

PARABLE OF THE CONVERT

A dialogue between a recent convert and an unbelieving friend:

"So you have been converted to Christ?"
"Yes."
"Then you must know a great deal about him. Tell me: What country was he born in?"
"I don't know."
"What was his age when he died?"
"I don't know."
"How many sermons did he preach?"
"I don't know."
"You certainly know very little for a man who claims to be converted to Christ!"

"You are right. I am ashamed at how little I know about him.
But this much I do know: Three years ago I was a drunkard. I was in debt. My family was falling to pieces. My wife and children would dread my return home each evening. But now I have given up drink; we are out of debt; ours is now a happy home. All this Christ has done for me. This much I know of him!"

PROFILES

Creative Communicators

BISHOP ROBIN LEAMY, S.M.: who played Olympic Rugby for New Zealand, met our flight at 4:30 a.m. with smiles, hugs, and a ton of flower leis, and later took me to the cleaners on the tennis court. Bishop Bob is a superb communicator and when he is not traveling by boat to some of the many islands in his far-flung diocese, he keeps in touch by shortwave radio telephone.

SR. ALLISON: with help from Sisters Kathy, Margaret, Julie and Natalia— keeps an eye on the communications room and cassette resource library: both to support their teaching in the Catholic School—and to support the radio media ministry. H

ENRICA WILSON, DAVE and MARYANNE MACINTOSH: of over 12 apostles of Catholic Communication in Rarotonga; they produce for local radio: the Mass, home prayer, interviews and documentaries—as well as training. Simple, unaffected, deeply involved with the poor — lived for 7 years with homeless in the dirt under a bridge — and use a popular column in the secular newspapers to tell parables of contemporary justice and injustice.

TAHITI

A T A GLANCE   *TAHITI*
Population: *95,000*
Capital: *Papeete*
Language: *Polynesian dialect, French, English*
Faith Expression: *Christianity, Buddhism, Confucianism*
Currency: *Pacific financial community franc (PFC Franc)*

SOCIETY IS.

Tahiti

polynesie francaise

POSTES
"PEINTURE SUR TAPA"
RF

TAHITI 1969

POSTCARD
REFLECTIONS

Look at those hats . . . !

P.S.—The dance worked . . . it rained all day in Papeete! Quel Dommage!

Papeete is the Big Bay just behind the airport—the parish "Maria No Te Hau" and Diocesan Center and fabulous audio and video studios (3 cameras! etc.!!!) are on the edge of the village—wow.

In a hotel room:

The manager has personally passed all the water served here.

Watched a beautiful sunset (ce soir) through the stained glass windows of the Cathedral while we concelebrated the 6pm Saturday evening Mass with the Communication Director, Father Paul. The following day met with Bishop Michel at the Media Center.

PARABLE OF GUILT

The Master was always teaching that guilt is an evil emotion to be avoided like the very devil—all guilt.

"But are we not to hate our sins?" a disciple said one day.

"When you are guilty, it is not your sins you hate but yourself."

EASTER ISLAND

EASTER ISLAND

Well, here we were on Easter Island in the middle of Lent—and also the middle of the Pacific! The 1/2 hr. tour of Easter Island and its famous stone statues is only for folks going to Tahiti from Chile (did the reverse). What's the difference you ask and the cuties who came out to greet us give you your answer!

POSTCARD
REFLECTIONS

These guys are stoned—with hats to match—thank heaven my itinerary calling for a 24-hour layover was wrong— nothing soft and warm here but the sun. I was glad to reboard our tiny (6 across) Lan Chile Jet, even if my next seat neighbor passed out!

186

CONTRACT WITH GOD

I loved teaching media ministry on the South Pacific Islands, but I missed "home": where your heart is, and your pillow and shower and icebox and books and phone and food and language and culture and family and friends, where they have to take you in and try to love you.

A year on the road made my heart grow fonder and more appreciative of the many things and folks we take for granted, like the communicators and the Chancery office staff who have been my working family for the last 11 years.

All this gushy nostalgia reminds me of my annual contract with God. Some years ago the priests of the Archdiocese of San Francisco, with bodies, feelings, minds and souls, took the Ministry to Priests Program and agreed to make and renew each year a personal contract with God. This private covenant, or agreement, covers the basics of human need and growth: physical, emotional, intellectual and spiritual. Once a year I sit down quietly with God and write down what I need to work on during the coming year.

In the physical area, for example, I have learned something new about myself after my year of travel. I always thought I needed only five to six hours' sleep a night. I was wrong. I need eight! So this year's contract with God calls for more sleep. Something else I discovered: I've always assumed I was a 165-pounder. But this global pilgrimage has taken off 20 pounds, and I'm much happier and healthier physically. As you habitual dieters know, it's not only losing 20 pounds of ugly flab, but tightening and strengthening what's there. Are you beginning to get creative ideas for your own contract with God?

Take the second area: the emotional the psychological. What is your biggest need or lack here? Mine is for quality time to "waste" with family and friends. I need homes, including priests' houses, where I can let down what's left of my hair. We all need the same emotional essentials: laughter and love. Where there is laughter and love there is mental health. Where either is missing there is disease. How do you know if you're getting enough laughs and loving? We all need 32 laughs and 9 hugs a day! I would have died from emotional starvation if it hadn't been for the loving open-door, open-arm hospitality of brother priests and sisters all around the world. I've never been so proud and pleased to be a Catholic—and a priest.

We're not just bodies, sensate temples of the Holy Spirit. We also have an intellect. Am I feeding and exercising and loving my mind? With what? Books, plays, movies, games, puzzles, classes, seminars? Many of the countries I visited this year do not have television yet—or couch potatoes. It's amazing to see families who still talk to one another during dinner, who read and play games together. What is the last challenging book you read or adult education course you attended? Don't contract with God to ban television. Promise God you will build in time for intellectual stimulation. Make your promise realistic, reasonable and rewarding, and stick with it.

Which brings us to the big one: the spiritual—for me, prayer. The breviary, the daily, universal prayer of the one, holy, catholic, apostolic Church—our everyday worldwide pray-a-thon— is always in this part of my contract with God. The loneliness and aloneness helped me rediscover the calming contemplation of this liturgy of the hours—which reportedly happens to every priest as he matures—but I want to focus especially on prayer as communication, which begins with listening. For years I have done all the talking in prayer: "Let us pray . . . " and then we read or speak or dream—and God can't get a word in edgewise. This year's spiritual contract calls for quiet time at the beginning and end of every day: for active listening to God. "Let us pray . . . let us communicate . . . let us listen."

This started off as a thank-you note—and look how I've rambled. Well, that's what happens when you're homesick: your mind wanders almost as much as your body.

South America

Caribbean Sea

North Atlantic Ocean

Caracas•

VENEZUELA

•Bogota

COLOMBIA

PERU

BRAZIL

•Lima

BOLIVIA

•La Paz

Sao Paulo•

South Pacific Ocean

Santiago•

Buenos Aires•

ARGENTINA

CHILE

South Atlantic Ocean

VENEZUELA

A T A GLANCE   **VENEZUELA**
Population: 19,246,000
Capital With Population: Caracas 2,700,000
Language: Spanish
Literacy: 86%
Faith Expression: Roman Catholic 96%
Currency Used: Bolivar
Cities I Visited: Caracas, Mérida

VENEZUELA

POSTCARD
REFLECTIONS

Arrived Caracas Simon Bolivar Airport 5 am, jogged thru early mist & flew up here (400 Mi.) into the Andes, to Mérida, a University town, where church owns TV/radio stations & daily paper, for our 3-day workshop—but riots broke out, so we 'hid' in priest's family home for 2 days & good friends got us back on a plane to Caracas. Guns shooting —many dead—pray!

*It's hard to appreciate Venezuela in this stage of popular uprising and military/police curfew and suspension of constitutional freedoms and guarantees—Thousands are believed killed (hundreds reported) and tension/terror reign . . . We could hear the gunfire from our windows—Yes, it certainly was an adventure! Also an unforgettable **LENT**.*

In the lobby of a hotel across from a Russian Orthodox monastery:

> You are welcome to visit the cemetery where famous Russian and Soviet composers, artists, and writers are buried daily except Thursday.

PARABLE OF SELF TRANSFORMATION

To a disciple who was forever complaining about others the Master said, "If it is peace you want, seek to change yourself, not other people. It is easier to protect your feet with slippers than to carpet the whole of the earth."

PROFILES

Creative Communicators

DR. JERRY O'SULLIVAN: deeply spiritual, intelligent, sensitive professional, Ph.D. in Communications (Stanford University), offers job training for the poor and marginated, and directs the Venezuelan Bishops Communications Department on pastoral videos, educommunication and media awareness. The Catholic Church in Venezuela owns 3 local TV stations, 8 radio stations and 4 of the 7 daily Catholic newspapers in Latin America. Jerry is a genius at balancing: working with alternative community media for evangelization—and also serving as advisor to the Latin America Bishops Conference (DECOS-CELAM) and the Pontifical Council for Social Communications. Jerry and his wife Freda and their young daughters Geraldine and Edel gave me sanctuary—and delicious Irish hospitality—in their home in the Caracas hills during one of Venezuela's violent revolutions.

191

COLOMBIA

AT A GLANCE   **COLOMBIA**
Population: 31,821,000
Capital With Population: *Bogota 4,900,000*
Language: *Spanish*
Literacy: *82%*
Faith Expression: *Roman Catholic (95%)*
Currency Used: *Colombian Peso*
Cities I Visited: *Bogota*

COLOMBIA

Checked into Room 1255 with a magnificent view of the freeway—but at least there was no gunfire, curfew or revolucion as in Venezuela! Viva la libertad!

Main product: coffee (mas suave que Brazil); real main product: drugs (has terrible reputation for theft, robbery and tourist bashing . . . but it's not the drugs—they don't take the drugs themselves: they're making too much $ supplying the rest of the world). Second main product: flowers (esp. roses!) Happy Ending!

POSTCARD
REFLECTIONS

This is the real Bogota—no, the people are the real Bogota and they're just like these squat streets, dark rough houses, tiled, balconied and matched to their mountains!

192

Smiles to go

In a hotel catering to skiers:

Not to perambulate the corridors in the hours of repose in the boots of ascension.

Checked into the Tequendama Hotel, took a siesta, went for a jog up the mountain, and 'Santa Maria' led me right to her Plaza De Toros—where the 3:30 pm Corrida was just beginning. I enjoyed the most exciting, magnificent bullfight in many years! . . .Well, what else do you do on a Sunday afternoon in Colombia after Mass?

PROFILES

Creative Communicators

PADRE PEDRO BRISEÑO CHAVEZ, S.S.P.:
outgoing, smart, good organizer as Executive Secretary of DECOS-CELAM, Latin America Bishops Communications Conference, who knows how to serve both "churches" in Latin America:
the church of position, prestige and ecclesiastical structure and the church of the poor, people-power and *comunidades de base*. Some waste energy warring against each other, the more creative discover ways to cooperate. Padre Pedro works closely with the Communications Episcopal Chairman Bishop Rosa Chavez (Auxiliary Bishop of San Salvador in Centro America) who is also a Catholic Communicator of deep faith, more interested in building bridges than fortresses.

COLOMBIA

BROTHER ALEJANDRO MEJÍA:
kind, gracious, creative producer and coordinator of AV materials (especially radio dramas and documentaries) for **SERTA**L: production for Latin American Bishops Conference.

JESUIT PADRES GABRIEL JAIME PEREZ AND JOAQUIN SANCHEZ:
most respected professors of Bogota's Universidad Javeriana communication and offered cordial collaboration—unfortunately the week I spent in Bogota, government troops lined the streets downtown and surrounded the University, preventing our meeting.

I have now climbed three great mountains (all taking about 1 1/2 hours!): Hong Kong was the most dramatic, Rarotonga the most difficult—and Bogota's Monserrate the most spiritual and beautiful. Blessings from above!

Spent a great day with the Bishops Conference, DECOS-CELAM, which guides all Catholic Communication in Latin America and with SERTAL which coordinates all productions—very interesting . . . then to find my hat "sombrero típico recuerdo" before departing for Lima early next a.m.

The bells are ringing: calling Latin Americans to a church whose outreach is greater than its grasp—& calling the Church back to the people!

PARABLE OF THE MIDDLE DISTANCE

Again and again the Master would be seen to discourage his disciples from depending on him, for this would prevent them from contacting the inner Source.

He was often heard to say, "Three things there are that when too close are harmful, when too far are useless and are best kept at middle distance: fire, the government and the guru."

PERU

AT A GLANCE   **PERU**
Population: 21,792,000
Capital With Population: Lima 4,330,000
Language: Spanish, Quechua, Aymara
Literacy: 79%
Faith Expression: Roman Catholic (90%)
Currency Used: Sol
Cities I Visited: Lima, Cusco

POSTCARD
REFLECTIONS

Went out for orientation dinner with 3 padres who had been here as missionaries for a combined total of 90 years! Wow, was I oriented!

This is what downtown Lima looks (and feels!) like all the time— when they're not having a procession, the **ambulantes** (street sellers) are turning downtown into a moving open market. (It's illegal!)

Calle Mira Calcetas, Cusco

Peru, too, is on the edge of financial collapse and violent revolution! I spent 3 hours in this plaza watching a strike (2 months long!) of government workers in front of the Cathedral— with military shock troops keeping peace with tanks shooting water like fire hoses! We all got a little wet.

... and you thought Safeway on Saturday was bad! ...

FR. GEORGE FLYNN: no-nonsense dedicated professional and one of the top missionary communicators in the church worldwide . . . wrote recently: *The situation in Peru is not good. As a matter of fact it is the worst that I have seen it in my 31 years here. People have gotten to accept as normal what used to be outrageous—regular blackouts, food shortages, no medicine, strikes, riots, bombings and daily assassinations by several different terrorist groups. Due to a postal strike we have had no mail for more than two months. The present government is hopelessly incompetent, confused and unbelievably corrupt. The currency exchange is out of control. In one week the rate has jumped from 8,500 peruvian "intis" to the U.S. dollar up to 14,000 to the dollar! As usual the poor—and that includes just about everybody here—are the ones that suffer the most. Keep Peru in your prayers. The people have been badly served. They deserve better.*

There are 4 types of Llama:
  1. Vicuña: grown small, fine wool
  2. Alpaca: bigger, fatter, more wool
  3. Tanaco: almost extinct
  4. Llamas: best, biggest (small pony)—carry heavy loads, waste serves as burning charcoal, bones for sewing and meat for eating!
The stones in the background are very deliberately jig-sawed to withstand earthquakes.

PERU

IDEAS IN MEDIA MINISTRY

CREATIVE
COMMUNICATING

PROSAN

Fr. George's approach for the last 15 years has been PROSAN: As a member of St. James' Missionary Society (Boston, Mass.) he produces 5 weekly programs for radio stations throughout Peru:

1. LA IGLESIA EN EL MUNDO DE HOY: Un noticiero católico tipo radio revista.

2. EVANGELIO DOMINICAL: Lectura del evangelio de la misa dominical con una breve catequesis sobre el evangelio y música sacra. Tiempo 12 minutos.

3. QUECHUA DOMINICAL: Evangelio dominical de la semana, sermon e himnos, todo en quechua sur andino. Tiempo 14 minutos.

4. EL PROVINCIANO: Variedades de informes tipo desarrollo humano con pautas y consejos utiles sobre agricultura, zootécnica, cocina, medicina, vida cívica, higiene. Tiempo 14 minutos.

5. LA MÚSICA DE AHORA Y DE SIEMPRE: Programa cultural con la mejor música del mundo y de toda epoca y estilo. Contiene además de la amplia selección de música mencionada, una intervención cultural y una moraleja cristiana. Tiempo 26 minutos.

We toured these famous Inca Empire Ruins dating back ages before 12th century (completely overlooked by the Spanish Conquistadores in 15th–16th centuries: rediscovered by Yale's Hiram Bingham in 1911!) but that huge mountain in the clouds was too much of a temptation—I left the group, and scaled the heights & saw God!

MACHUPICCHU

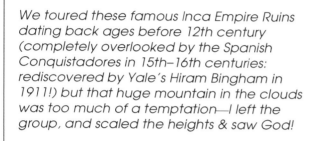

We learned how alike human beings have been for centuries— insecure, frightened, working like crazy to organize themselves, using architecture to protect, to beautify, using herbs to heal, using crises to create and grow, always believing in God and in their families and the future!

PARABLE OF THE TIGER AND THE FOX

A man walking through the forest saw a fox that had lost its legs and wondered how it lived. Then he saw a tiger come in with game in its mouth. The tiger had its fill and left the rest of the meat for the fox.

The next day God fed the fox by means of the same tiger. The man began to wonder at God's greatness and said to himself, "I too shall just rest in a corner with full trust in the Lord and he will provide me with all I need."

He did this for many days but nothing happened, and he was almost at death's door when he heard a voice say, "O you who are in the path of error, open your eyes to the truth! Follow the example of the tiger and stop imitating the disabled fox."

BOLIVIA

A T A GLANCE   **BOLIVIA**
Population: *6,876,000*
Capital With Population: *La Paz 955,000, Sucre 65,000*
Language: *Spanish, Quechua (34%), Aymara (25%)*
Literacy: *75%*
Faith Expression: *Roman Catholic (95%)*
Currency Used: *Bolivian Peso*
Cities I Visited: *La Paz*

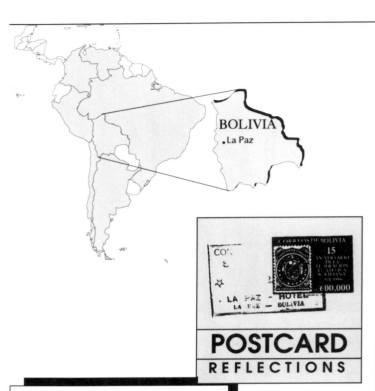

POSTCARD
REFLECTIONS

In North America the 'poor' are those who lack things like food, housing, clothing, education, freedom, opportunity, justice! In South America, the 'poor' are those who lack love.

One of the most beautiful cards, from one of the most naturally beautiful cities in the world! The snow capped Andes are near eternal and one girl compared the lights at night to the jewel-sparkles on a new bride's veil. "I've been to the mountain top . . . I've seen the promised land!"

I think my lungs and heart were made for this altitude—I felt high all the time: like flying in the clouds, outside the airplane—it gave rather than sapped my strength!

ERBOL

ERBOL is a brilliant network of educational community radio stations—with names like **Esperanza**, **Juan XXIII**, **Fides**, **San Gabriel**, and **Pio XII**—which use broadcast education, follow-up pamphlets and on-site workshops and festivals to help the poor and pre-literate campesinos improve their work, their families and their lives. Simple and successful! The world and the church could use many more ERBOLS or Educatión Radiofónica!

ERBOL's thirteen Catholic radio stations provide grass roots Educación Radiofónica through the creation of 9 types of programs:

- information
- catechesis and evangelization
- history, geography, cultural values
- agriculture and technology
- health, nutrition, and hygiene
- civics and leadership
- community development and economy
- basic education
- literacy

IDEAS IN MEDIA MINISTRY

CREATIVE
COMMUNICATING

PROFILES
Creative Communicators

PADRE HUGO ARA, S.J.:
young, energetic, priestly, gifted—I was finally able to track down this creative dynamo at the La Paz Municipal Theatre where he was directing a production of "The Man From La Mancha"—Secretary of Communication for the National Episcopal Conference by day and director of musical theatre by night—obviously my kind of communicator!

RONALD GREBE LOPEZ:
amazingly well organized, thoughtful and fruitful Executive Secretary of ERBOL, one of the most fascinating and productive multimedia ministries in the world.

FR. GENE TOLAND, FR. PAUL NEWPOWER, BROTHER DAVID, et alia:
in the world-renown tradition of Maryknoll hospitality these missionaries offer warm welcome to their almost-two-mile-high La Paz Maryknoll House (nicknamed "The Ice Palace") and, as part of their missionary outreach to the people, produce superb little 15-minute "Eduvideos"—most often personal profiles and documentaries of the local folk and faith, culture and church.

PARABLE OF THE MOON

"Don't look for God," the Master said. *"Just look—and all will be revealed."*
"But how is one to look?"
"Each time you look at anything, see only what is there and nothing else."
The disciples were bewildered, so the Master made it simpler: "For instance: When you look at the moon, see the moon and nothing else."
"What else could one see except the moon when one looks at the moon?"
"A hungry person could see a ball of cheese. A lover, the face of his beloved."

CHILE

A T A GLANCE   **CHILE**
Population: *12,866,000*
Capital With Population: *Santiago 4,858,000*
Language: *Spanish*
Literacy: *90%*
Faith Expression: *Predominantly Roman Catholic (89%),*
        Protestant (11%)
Currency Used: *Chilean Peso*
Cities I Visited: *Santiago*

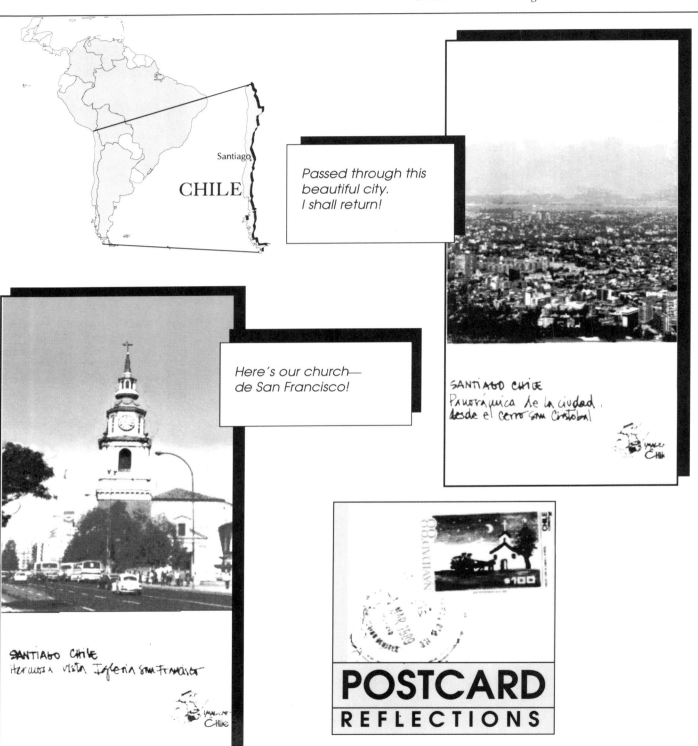

Passed through this beautiful city. I shall return!

SANTIAGO CHILE
Panorámica de la ciudad, desde el cerro San Cristóbal

Here's our church— de San Francisco!

SANTIAGO CHILE
Hermosa vista Iglesia San Francisco

POSTCARD
REFLECTIONS

MIGUEL ESPINOZA PAVEZ: cordial editor/writer for Chile's Episcopal Conference and **J. FRANCISCO CONTRERAS**: efficient, effective Director of Communications for the Chilean Bishops focus on several specific programs:

- educational workshops: for the pastoral use of mass media
- public relations: two-way communication between the bishops and the Chilean community
- publications: most notably, SERVICIO which tracks the Church's ministry in Chile—and lists new books in the Conferences' Pastoral Library.

IDEAS IN MEDIA MINISTRY

Videoteca Cultural is a video cassette library on "videocoop" with over 75 pastoral and cultural programs on video cassettes which are offered for special prices to members of the "Chile-Videocoop."

One of the most unusual and useful workshops took place in Santiago: a day-long media conference for liturgists and technicians on the challenge of broadcasting worship—or how do we pray via radio and television. Both the liturgy specialists and the media pros came together to educate each other in a common, enriching dialog.

CREATIVE
COMMUNICATING

PARABLE OF AWARENESS

"Is salvation obtained through action or through meditation?"
"Through neither. Salvation comes from seeing."
"Seeing what?"
"That the gold necklace you wish to acquire is hanging round your neck. That the snake you are so frightened of is only a rope on the ground."

ARGENTINA

AT A GLANCE — **ARGENTINA**
Population: 32,617,000
Capital With Population: Buenos Aires
  2,900,000
Language: Spanish
Literacy: 94%
Faith Expression: Roman Catholic (92%)
Currency Used: Austral
Cities I Visited: Buenos Aires

POSTCARD
REFLECTIONS

One nite we processed from the Cathedral
down the main Avenida to this huge
square where (on a high rise fountain just to
the lower left of this photo!) they
re-enacted the last five stations of the cross
(we prayed the first 9 in procession) and
Jesus' crucifixion most powerfully.

Smiles to go

In a hotel elevator:

To move the cabin, push button for wishing floor. If the cabin should enter more persons, each one should press number of wishing floor. Driving is then going alphabetically by national order.

La Crujía

ARGENTINA

TELMO MEIRONE:
large, powerful, persuasive, charismatic Director of LA CRUJÍA, Center for Educational Communication, which offers workshops and radio-TV production courses, research, publications and methodologies to help church leaders see themselves as communicators.

OSVALDO HIRSHMAN:
well read, well traveled, well connected secretary for the World Association of Christian Communicators in Latin America—knows the key contacts, has good judgment, valuable experience and vision.

IDEAS IN MEDIA MINISTRY

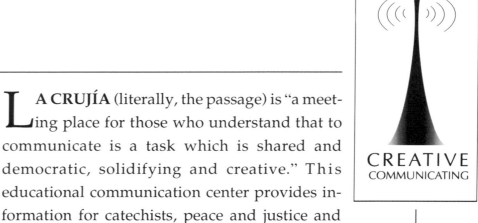

CREATIVE
COMMUNICATING

LA CRUJÍA (literally, the passage) is "a meeting place for those who understand that to communicate is a task which is shared and democratic, solidifying and creative." This educational communication center provides information for catechists, peace and justice and youth workers, and diocesan personnel. In addition to their workshops and seminars, research and publications, they also produce radio shows (like "Encuentros," a 5-minute daily humorous radio theatre where the Bible comes alive in modern characters—and funny characters). Their "Grupo Cooperativo" ("creators of Christian images") has completed scripting and seeks funds to produce a video documentary series entitled "Prophets In Our Time."

La Crujía es un lugar de encuentro para quienes entienden que comunicar es una tarea participativa, democrática, solidaria y creativa.

PARABLE OF THE FISH

The Master was strolling with some of his disciples along the bank of a river.

He said, "See how the fish keep darting about wherever they please. That's what they really enjoy."

A stranger overhearing that remark said, "How do you know what fish enjoy? You're not a fish."

The disciples gasped at what they took for impudence. The Master smiled at what he recognized as a fearless spirit of inquiry.

He replied affably, "And you, my friend, how do you know I am not a fish? You are not I."

The disciples laughed, taking this to be a well-deserved rebuff. Only the stranger was struck by its depth. All day he pondered it, then came to the monastery to say, "Maybe you are not as different from the fish as I thought. Or I from you."

We have brothers and sisters we haven't even met yet.

BRAZIL

A T A GLANCE — BRAZIL

Population: 153,992,000
Capital With Population: Brasilia 410,000
Language: Portuguese, English
Literacy: 76%
Faith Expression: Roman Catholic (89%), Protestant (7%)
Currency Used: Cruzeiro, New Cruzada
Cities I Visited: Sao Paulo, Rio de Janeiro

POSTCARD
REFLECTIONS

This **is** Sao Paulo!
15,000,000 downtown and
20 million in the greater
Sao Paulo area . . .

This was my little morning jogging
square—after a morning prayer visit
to the Cathedral. Early in the a.m.
there are hundreds of transients and
poor families just waking up from a
night on the cold cement.

Will you look at those waves!

PADRE CONRADO BERNING, S.V.D:
wise, committed founder and director of **Verbo Filmes** (10 years ago) to make film—now also video and audio cassettes— to help the church serve the poor and to help the poor help themselves. With a 16 or 35 mm camera hoisted on one shoulder Padre Conrado is off in a neighbor's car to document the plight and struggle of the poor in Sao Paolo—and then use the AV media to educate folks on both sides of the struggle.

RIO

This was my morning jogging trail—two main beaches: Copacabana and Ipanema—not bad!

209

BRAZIL

My favorite view was looking back and up from the beach, over the mountain range of 20-story hotels and through the forest of TV antennae, to Corcovado and Cristo, rising high in the heavens.

. . . and you will see the Lord in the clouds, coming on the air . . . and he will say: 'Peace, My Peace I Give To You' . . .

. . . with love and blessings from Cristo Redentor risen to embrace the world and from Miles who can't wait to see you!

PARABLE OF LIBERATION

"How shall I get liberation?"

"Find out who has bound you," said the Master.

The disciple returned after a week and said, "No one has bound me."

"Then why ask to be liberated?"

That was a moment of enlightenment for the disciple, who suddenly became free.

There are many prisons—which require many kinds of "liberation."

EPIJOG

Someone suggested calling this book: "Jogging with Jesus" because I went jogging every morning and used that 4–6 miles and 40–60 minutes as both my morning meditation and a valuable time to reflect on the experiences of yesterday and prepare for the workshops and challenges of the day.

For you other runners and walkers, here are some of the trails I tried—with the rating I assigned to each at the time. Fortunately, I was staying not at the downtown hotels but with families and with clergy who could direct me to the best routes and paths—especially in developing countries where the people do not jog, because they are hungry and need to conserve every calorie they can.

JOGGER'S SCORE CARD

CITIES (Chronologically)	TRAIL	RATING	CITIES (Chronologically)	TRAIL	RATING
Oxford	River Run	10	Dhaka	N.D. College Field	7
Hatch End (England)	Country Roads	5	Calcutta	Around Church	6
Rome	Villa Borghese	8	Madras	Sea Front	8
Turino	Town Square	5	Bangalore	City Park	9
Lyon	Country Roads	6	Hyderabad	Open Field	8
Munich	English Tea Garten	7	Bombay	Shoreline	9
Paris	Bois de Bologne	7	Goa	Ft. Aguada Beach	10
Brussels	City Streets	5	Cochin	County Roads	6
Baarn (Netherlands)	Soccer Field	7	Singapore	Ft. Canning and Waterfront	10
Copenhagen	Canal Paths	8	Bali	Roadside and Beach	9
Honolulu	Beach	9	Johor (Malaysia)	Roadways	6
Apia (Samoa)	Beach	8	Jakarta	Suburban Streets	7
Wellington	Hills	7	Yogyakarta	Rice Fields	8
Melbourne	Park	9	Surabaya	Mountain Top	9
Harare (Zimbabwe)	City Streets	5	Sydney	Parks	7
Blantyre (Malawi)	Coffee Fields	6	Suva (Fiji)	Beach Road	9
Lilongwe (Malawi)	Back Roads	6	Goroka (PNG)	Coffee Orchard	9
Lusaka (Zambia	Golf Course	8	Rarotonga (The Cooks)	Needle Mt. Top	10
Livingston	Country Trails	6	Papeete (Tahiti)	Oceanside Road	7
Mombasa	Sandy Beach	10	Caracas	Suburban Hills	8
Nairobi	Back Streets	8	Bogota	Montserate	9
Monrovia (Liberia)	Sea Front	7	Lima	Miraflores Oceanside	9
Freetown (Sierra Leone)	Beach	6	Cusco	Mountain Top	8
Seoul	River Bed	8	Machu Picchu	Mountain Top	9
Tokyo	Emperor's Palace	9	La Paz	Hillside Paths	8
Taipei	College Track	10	Santiago	La Virgen Mount	9
Hong Kong	Furnicular Mt. Top	10+	Buenos Aires	Docks and Waterfront	7
Beijing	Back Streets	8	Sao Paolo	Cathedral Square	6
Macau	Mountain Roads	9	Rio de Janeiro	Ipanema and Copacabana	9
Bangkok	City Park Trails	10			

As I Grow

Please...

Understand that I am growing up and changing very fast. It must be difficult to keep pace with me, but please try.

Listen to me and give me brief, clear answers to my questions. Then I will keep sharing my thoughts and feelings.

Reward me for telling the truth. Then I am not frightened into lying.

Tell me when you make mistakes and what you learned from them. Then I can accept that I am OK, even when I blunder.

Pay attention to me, and spend time with me. Then I can believe that I am important and worthwhile.

Do the things you want me to do. Then I have a good, positive model.

Trust and respect me. Even though I am smaller than you, I have feelings and needs just like you.

Compliment and appreciate me. Then I'll feel good, and I'll want to continue to please you.

Help me explore my unique interests, talents and potential. In order for me to be happy, I need to be me, and not just someone you want me to be.

Be an individual and create your own happiness. Then you can teach me the same, and I can live a happy, successful and fulfilling life.

Thank you for hearing me, I love you!

Compliments of Highlights® for Children

911180